# BUILDING THE AI BANK

## Speed, Judgement and Power

Emmanuel Daniel



notionpress.com

INDIA • SINGAPORE • MALAYSIA

ISBN

Hardcase 979-8-90362-873-5
Paperback 979-8-90342-316-3

# Contents

*Forewords* ........ *9*

*Preface: When speed defines the rules* ........ *15*

**Chapter 1 The World after Digital Banks** ........ **21**

From Digital to Delegation ........ 22

From Platforms to Agents ........ 23

Generative AI and the Customer's Narrative ........ 25

Web3 Is Not Web 3.0 ........ 26

Why AI, CeFi, DeFi, and TradFi Must Be Read Together ........ 28

**Chapter 2 Where is AI Taking Us?** ........ **31**

Decentralising Intelligence ........ 32

When the User Defines the Context ........ 34

The Shift from Language to Action ........ 35

Ambient Finance and the End of the Device ........ 36

Navigating the Path of Least Resistance ........ 38

**Chapter 3 Building the AI Operating Model** ........ **39**

Who owns the decisions? ........ 41

Measuring the right matrix ........ 42

A Note to Digital-Only Banks ........ 44

Execution Beyond the Institution ........ 45

**Chapter 4 The Balance Sheet Comes to Life .................. 47**
AI as a Balance-Sheet Amplifier ............................................ 49
Treasury in a Game of Thrones ............................................. 50
When Treasury Goes Real-Time ............................................. 53
The Retail–Treasury FTP Tension ........................................... 54
Digital Assets on the Balance Sheet ........................................ 56
Programmable Liabilities and Active Stability ....................... 57
US State Banks Already Living This ........................................ 57

**Chapter 5 Payments as AI in Motion .............................. 59**
From Messaging to Execution ................................................ 60
Cross-Border CBDC Pilots ..................................................... 62
Permissioned versus permissionless ......................................... 66
Payments in an Agent-Mediated World .................................. 67
The legacy card players ........................................................... 68
PayPal and Stripe: Two Diverging AI Futures ....................... 70
Can India's UPI scale intelligence? .......................................... 70
China: The state versus agentic AI tension ............................ 71
M-Pesa: From Mobile Money to AI Infrastructure .............. 74

**Chapter 6 AI as an Operating System .............................. 75**
The Real AI Stack of a Bank .................................................. 76
Models Do Not Create Power ................................................ 80
Execution: Where Payments Change Everything .................. 81
The Data Outside the Bank .................................................... 82
Why Ring-Fencing Fails in an AI World ................................ 84
Trust Becomes Machine-Readable .......................................... 84

**Chapter 7 New Products for a New Age ........................ 87**

Ghosts from A Digital Past ........................ 88

Digital Assets Are Not Products Either ........................ 92

"The Conversation is the Product" ........................ 92

Reddit and the Pre-Product Signal ........................ 94

Products as life management ........................ 95

Products Ruled by Permissions ........................ 97

The Product Strategy of the AI Bank ........................ 98

**Chapter 8 Agents from Apps to Actors ........................ 101**

From Tools to Actors ........................ 102

Generative AI and Agents Feed Each Other ........................ 104

Agents Inside Financial Institutions Today ........................ 105

Outside Banking, the Pattern Is Clear ........................ 106

Customers Are Building Agents Too ........................ 106

The Balance-Sheet Consequence ........................ 108

From APIs to Execution Partners ........................ 109

Agents Redefine Organisational Boundaries ........................ 109

Can AI Agents Become an AI Bank? ........................ 110

**Chapter 9 Risk, Regulation and Networked Belief ........ 113**

Risk was Labour Intensive ........................ 114

From Risk as Exposure to Risk as Behaviour ........................ 115

From Basel I to Basel III: Risk as Position ........................ 116

Basel V: Risk as Behaviour in Motion ........................ 118

The CRO's roles are already changing ........................ 120

Manufactured Belief as a New Risk ........................ 122

Human Discretion Repositioned ....................................................123
Financial Inclusion and Network Risk...................................124
Risk as Legitimacy in the AI Bank.........................................125

**Chapter 10 Cybersecurity in the Age of Intelligence ...... 127**
When Identity Collapses ..........................................................127
Cyber Is No Longer a Perimeter.............................................128
Zero Trust Architecture Meets Reality...................................129
Vendor Concentration .............................................................130
Protocol Risk Becomes Operational Risk ..............................131
From Preventing Fraud to Surviving Deception..................132
Cybersecurity as a Learning System.......................................132
What AI Banks Must Do Differently.....................................133

**Chapter 11 Ethics is in the Plumbing.............................. 135**
From Principles to Power ........................................................136
Bias and Discrimination ..........................................................137
Explainability Is a Moral Boundary........................................138
Surveillance, Privacy and Consent are Design Questions.......138
Automation Bias and Abdicated Responsibility ..................139
Manipulation and Behaviour Steering ...................................140
Unequal Error Distribution Reveals Who Ethics Serves.........................................................................140
Speed Without Due Process Is the New Ethical Failure Mode.................................................................141
Model Bias, Drift, and Silent Value Change..........................141
Ethics as Infrastructure............................................................142

**Chapter 12 Leadership When Machines Decide............. 143**

When Leadership Becomes Explicit....................................144

What Boards Are Really Asking..........................................144

The First Reframe: AI Is Not a Project Line Item ..............145

Should We Abandon Digital Banking?................................146

Leadership Roles Under Pressure ......................................147

The Second Reframe: Invest in Decision Surfaces, Not Scale ...............................................................148

A Board Heuristic for the AI Bank ....................................149

The Final Reframe: AI Spend Is a Statement of Intent..........149

**Chapter 13 Conclusion: A First Day at an AI Bank (2030).............................................151**

*Glossary* ........................................................................................*157*

*Index*..............................................................................................*165*

*References*......................................................................................*169*

*Bibliography*..................................................................................*177*

# Forewords

## Managing the tensions

In my own writings on AI Cognitive Dissonance — particularly in "AI's Silent Fracture: Reconciling Ambition with Execution" — the key issues in building an "AI Bank" stem from the deep tension between bold AI ambitions and the conservative, regulated realities of banking. Financial institutions crave rapid AI-driven innovation for competitive advantage, yet face demands for unbreakable stability, strict compliance, and minimal risk.

This dissonance appears in governance flip-flops (centralized vs. decentralized), talent boom-bust cycles, unstable AI leadership, massive hidden sunk costs, and excessive scrutiny on AI pilots — where tiny errors halt progress while legacy risks persist unchallenged.

These conflicts stall deployments, waste hundreds of millions, and limit sustainable ROI. Resolution demands embracing duality: parallel mandates, separate budgets, aligned incentives, and clear trade-offs between speed and reliability to enable trustworthy AI integration.

Emmanuel provides a clear-eyed view of how artificial intelligence is reshaping banking—not as an incremental tool, but as a fundamental shift in institutional design.

The book argues convincingly that AI inverts the traditional model: digital banking accelerated human rules through software, but

AI delegates judgment itself to systems that infer, adapt, and act autonomously. This creates an ecosystem where speed, network effects, and decentralized intelligence redefine who controls access, terms, pricing, and consequences.

As Emmanuel notes, banks risk becoming machine-supported intelligences that employ people, rather than the reverse. Most institutions remain unprepared, deploying AI while retaining governance suited to human discretion. The result can be accelerated decisions without matching accountability, as evidenced by events like the collapse of Silicon Valley Bank.

Leadership faces the hardest questions: AI is not a project or line item but a statement of institutional intent. Boards must prioritize decision surfaces over scale. Emmanuel draws from practical sources—boardroom dialogues, and emerging-market examples like WeBank, Nubank, and M-Pesa's evolution—where AI enters where human judgment cannot scale.

This book challenges bankers to design deliberately for an AI-native future or risk drifting into institutions they no longer control. It is essential reading for leaders navigating this transition, where trust, innovation, and accountability must align at machine speed.

**– David R. Hardoon,**

Global Head of AI Enablement, Standard Chartered Bank

February 2026

## Autonomous decision making is not an option

Emmanuel Daniel's *Building the AI Bank* offers a comprehensive and penetrating examination of a new paradigm in the banking industry—one that is transforming how banks must operate in the age of artificial intelligence. The opening chapters establish several foundational insights. While the balance sheet remains central to bank management, decision-making must now occur in real time. AI systems, operating within boundaries defined by leadership, will increasingly make autonomous decisions. The traditional, slower methods of managing a balance sheet are no longer sufficient.

A major strength of the book is its clear exposition of why autonomous AI decision-making is not optional but essential. AI must be empowered not only to predict outcomes but also to execute decisions across all levels of the institution. Practically, this requires leadership to overhaul information flows to enable effective real-time decision-making, while also establishing clear parameters around liquidity management, credit allocation, capital adequacy, and risk. Leadership can no longer operate within the confines of quarterly reporting cycles; instead, it must embrace continuous responsiveness and adaptive governance.

The book is dense with insight, presented in concise, impactful sections that invite reflection. Gradually, a compelling big picture emerges: AI-driven decision-making is dynamic and demands a fundamental redesign of a bank's core functions. Strategic plans are no longer static documents but are translated by AI into systems that learn, update, and act continuously.

This is essential reading for board members and treasury executives. Its themes should permeate the entire organization—from product development and marketing to compliance and ethics committees.

**– Anoop Rai,**

Professor of Finance, Frank G, Zarb School of Business,<br>
Hofstra University, New York<br>
February 2026

## Alignment with the customer's intent

I recently spoke to a private banker who noted that in these times, we cannot trust a single static decision. We must remain vigilant and "ride the waves" of the market, making decisions in real-time. This is also the essence of the AI journey.

We see this reinvention everywhere. In retail malls, AI now directs property care services to exactly where foot traffic is highest. AI kiosks translate complex requests for tourists instantly. Inside financial institutions, agents are already reviewing the performance of Relationship Managers, giving real-time "traffic light" guidance on customer interests and investment biases. Work itself is being reinvented. Complex, long-running tasks are being automated, freeing us to engage on a human level to ensure the right outcomes.

This brings us to the vital question this book answers: What, then, is an AI Bank?

As Emmanuel Daniel articulates in these pages, the AI Bank is a living institution where the balance sheet breathes, reacting to information and liquidity in real-time. It is an organization where judgement is delegated to machines, but accountability is firmly retained by leaders.

In this new era, the AI Bank does not just compete for attention; it competes for alignment with the customer's intent. It is an institution where agents negotiate value continuously, and where trust is not a static brand promise, but a real-time execution capability. This is the wake-up call retailers faced a decade ago: the realization that the barrier for a customer to leave had dropped to zero.

The race has begun. We must accept the challenge to rethink our organizations, moving rapidly toward a composable, AI-enabled infrastructure. We must build dynamic teams where human experts are paired with AI to drive high profitability. This book is the blueprint for that transformation—a guide to making Speed to Change and Speed to Trust the two currencies of the new bank.

**– Axel Winter,**
CEO, Pivot Digital & XPONENTIAL
(A Siam Piwat Group Company)
Former Global Chief Architect, Standard Chartered Bank
February 2026

## Hidden risks are scaling alongside

Emmanuel Daniel has written a very timely book. Banking is information-centric, so it should be no surprise that digital automation and artificial intelligence are having pervasive effects on the industry. Going forward, not every bank will be fully digital, of course, but all successful banks will find a way to exploit the revolutionary new toolkit. Daniel's book is loaded with pithy insights, each of which might be unpacked into a full book or essay of its own. A central challenge for innovating institutions will be managing the many tradeoffs inherent in technologies that are scaling both risks and returns exponentially. By now, we have all experienced the phenomenon of an AI chatbot cheerfully and confidently delivering a clearly false response to a query. Now imagine that chatbot is crafting your loan approvals. We've all had an infuriating conversation with an obtuse, AI-guided telephone response system that somehow can't address your question nor direct your call any further. Now imagine that AI agent is has become the chief point of contact for your best depositors. AI/digital banking works incredibly well, except when it doesn't. At a time when we don't yet fully understand the ramifications of these technologies, the shift to AI/digital banking can be a bit like playing high-stakes Russian roulette: new markets and the associated profits may scale quickly, but hidden risks will be scaling right alongside them. As Daniel emphasizes, a critical issue for innovating institutions will be to interleave these technologies into banking without losing sight of the many risks -- both novel and traditional -- that require deep judgment to manage well.

**– Mark Flood,**

Visiting Research Scholar, Center for Financial Policy,
University of Maryland February 2026

# Preface: When speed defines the rules

This book is not about artificial intelligence as a tool, a software upgrade, or the next productivity wave in banking. It is about the evolution of a whole new ecosystem where speed, the network effect and the lack of control over processes in AI will shape the future of banking.

Who gets access. On what terms. At what price. And with what consequences. For most of modern financial history, the power in banking was exercised by people through institutions, laws, and balance sheets. Judgement was human. Accountability was personal. Failure had a face.

Also, I have grounded this book in behavioural economics, network theory, and infrastructure governance — not fintech trend commentary.

The digital banking era changed the medium but not the logic. Judgement was translated into rules and embedded in software. Decisions travelled faster and at greater scale, but they were still recognisably human in origin. When systems failed, responsibility could still be traced back to a committee, a policy, or a senior executive who signed off.

The AI era breaks that continuity.

Artificial intelligence does not merely execute instructions. It infers, predicts, and adapts. It learns from data institutions do not fully control and from environments that change faster than governance cycles. Once judgement is delegated, even partially, the institution itself changes character. A bank stops being a collection of people supported by machines. It becomes a machine-supported intelligence that employs people.

Most banks are not prepared for this inversion.

They are deploying AI while clinging to governance models designed for human discretion. They are accelerating decision-making without redesigning accountability. They are optimising efficiency while quietly eroding legitimacy.

This is not a hypothetical concern. It is already visible.

When JP Morgan's Jamie Dimon warns in his annual shareholder letters that technology risk has become inseparable from business risk, he is not talking about chatbots or productivity tools[1]. He is talking about institutions whose internal decision speed no longer matches their governance speed.

When David Solomon discusses AI publicly, he returns repeatedly to accountability and decision authority rather than productivity[2]. Goldman Sachs is not confused about what is at stake: speed without ownership is institutional risk.

These are not futurists speaking. They are CEOs already managing institutions where judgement is leaking into systems faster than policies can follow.

The next failure in banking will not come from bad loans, cyberattacks, or fintech disruption alone. It will come from delegated intelligence without institutional design. From systems that optimise legally but fail institutionally. From speed without accountability.

We caught an early glimpse of this dynamic in the collapse of Silicon Valley Bank.

SVB did not fail because its assets were uniquely toxic. It failed because information moved faster than governance. Depositors reacted not to fundamentals, but to belief, amplified through digital channels. Liquidity evaporated in days. Committees convened too slowly. By the time humans reacted, the system had already decided.

AI would have compressed it further.

This is why it is tempting, and dangerous, to describe the AI Bank as simply the next phase of the digital bank.

The digital bank was an extension of the physical bank. It changed channels, interfaces, and cost structures. It did not change the nature of judgement. Humans still decided. Systems still executed.

The AI Bank is not an extension of the digital bank. It is a different institution. Judgement itself moves into the system. Decisions are no longer triggered only by humans, nor reviewed only after the fact. They are inferred, prioritised, and acted upon continuously and autonomously.

This distinction explains much of the resistance.

In the United States and Europe, incumbents worry about employees displaced by machines, fraud amplified by automation, and regulatory scrutiny. These are valid concerns. But they are not the core issue. The deeper risk lies in pretending that these changes can be absorbed without institutional redesign.

Some of the clearest early signals come from outside the traditional centres of banking power.

In Brazil, Nubank demonstrated that digital-first banking could be profitable at scale by redesigning onboarding, servicing, and decisioning for a mobile world[3]. But even Nubank did not redesign judgement itself. Its success illustrates the ceiling of the digital bank, not the arrival of the AI Bank.

In China, WeBank showed what happens when a bank is built as a high-frequency decision engine embedded into platform behaviour[4]. In South Korea, KakaoBank demonstrated how distribution, identity, and daily habits could be designed as one system[5]. These institutions rebuilt process and distribution. They did not fully redesign governance.

These examples are not romantic success stories. Many are messy. Some are fragile. A few are cautionary tales. But they share one truth: AI enters banking first where humans cannot scale judgement fast enough.

Much of what currently passes for "AI transformation" in developed markets misses this point.

Copilots, chat interfaces, and internal productivity tools are not useless. But they are largely theatre. They sit at the surface of the institution. They make organisations feel modern. They leave power exactly where it has always been.

The first industries to become meaningfully AI-native did not start with chat.

Pharmaceutical companies such as Moderna embedded AI into drug discovery, clinical trials, and manufacturing because decisions had to be made continuously under regulatory constraint[6]. Logistics firms like Amazon and Maersk embedded AI into routing and risk because execution never pauses[7]. Defence and intelligence platforms such as Palantir became AI-native by designing systems where decisions could be made, audited, reversed, and defended under pressure[8].

These organisations did not ask, "How do we use AI?"
They asked, "What decisions can no longer wait for humans?"
Banking is arriving late to that question, but with far higher stakes.

The investor community has begun to articulate this shift quite bluntly. Some argue that traditional banks are becoming *"value traps"* because their assets and business models are anchored to a linear past while the economy is being reshaped by exponential technologies. In their framing, book value becomes meaningless when assets are being stranded in real time by agentic-driven changes.

This book is grounded in practice. I drew my arguments from boardrooms, regulatory dialogues, simulation exercises and executive programmes across regions where demographic pressure, infrastructure constraints, and regulatory ambition collide most visibly. These environments act as stress tests for ideas that the industry cannot afford to postpone.

It may not be obvious at first, but I take the reader back to the balance sheet as to where the transformation must be captured. The traditional bank's balance has already morphed several times since the end of the Bretton Woods era, and it will transform yet again in the AI age.

The chapters in my book correspond to the structure an concerns of the traditional bank as we know it today, so that bankers will recognise the different parts of the institution as I discuss them. But the resulting organization that AI is creating is one that technically does not at all exist today.

Banks will either design themselves deliberately for an AI-native future, or drift into institutions they no longer fully understand themselves.

**Emmanuel Daniel**
January 2026

# CHAPTER ONE

# The World after Digital Banks

*"What looks like progress is often just speed."*
*– Yuval Noah Harari*[9]

---

Digital banking was never transformative.

It was translational.

Banks took analogue processes and rendered them in software. Forms became screens. Branches became apps. Clerks became workflows. Costs fell and convenience improved, but the architecture of banking remained intact. Humans decided. Systems executed.

This matters, because much of the current confusion about AI in banking comes from assuming it is simply the next phase of that same journey. It is not.

Artificial intelligence invites banks into a different universe.

When a system can infer intent from behaviour, price risk dynamically, negotiate terms in real time, and learn continuously from outcomes, decision-making is no longer an exclusively human domain. This is not an invitation to incrementally better analytics or automation. It is a structural shift in how judgement itself is exercised inside the institution.

The uncomfortable truth is that banks have been delegating judgement for decades.

Credit engines approve loans. Fraud systems block transactions. AML filters exclude customers. Limit systems enforce exposure constraints. Millions of decisions already occur without human intervention, often invisibly. Relationship managers intervene only at the edges.

What changes with AI is not the *fact* of delegation.
It is its nature.

Traditional models were narrow, static, and bounded. They operated within clearly defined domains and were reviewed periodically. AI systems are broader, adaptive, and increasingly interconnected. They form beliefs about customers, markets, and risks, and they update those beliefs continuously as new data arrives.

Once belief replaces rules, governance must change.

Institutions built to supervise deterministic systems cannot control probabilistic ones using the same committees, reporting cycles, and escalation thresholds. This is the point at which the digital bank reaches its limit.

## From Digital to Delegation

One of the most successful digital banks in the world, Nubank, began with a narrow wedge: credit cards for under-served customers frustrated by opaque pricing and indifferent service. Under the leadership of David Vélez, Nubank rebuilt onboarding, servicing, credit decisioning, and collections around the smartphone[10].

Nubank matters for one reason above all: it proved that digital-first banking could be profitable at scale. Not by putting branch products onto a screen, but by rebuilding the machinery behind the screen.

Much earlier in China, WeBank, backed by Tencent, demonstrated what happens when a bank is built as a high-frequency decision engine embedded directly into platform behaviour[11]. Credit assessment, pricing, and servicing were designed to operate at the cadence of e-commerce and messaging, not branches.

In South Korea, KakaoBank showed how distribution, identity, and daily financial habits could be designed as a single system[12]. Adoption came quickly because the bank lived inside the customer's existing digital life.

These institutions won by redesigning process and distribution. But this is also where their limits became visible. Digital banks optimised efficiency. They did not redesign judgement. That was for the AI Bank to perfect.

Credit decisions remained episodic. Liquidity was still managed in batches. Risk was monitored after the fact. Products were static, even if delivery was dynamic. Information was treated as exhaust rather than as a first-class economic asset.

It didn't help that regulators insisted that digital banks surrender their disruptor badge and be populated with retired bankers with credentials from the old world.

This is not a criticism. It is the limitations with which they operated.

Digital banks showed how far process redesign could go without rethinking how beliefs are formed, updated, and governed inside the institution. AI exposes that ceiling.

## From Platforms to Agents

In my first book, I discussed the personalisation of finance[13]. I was sure then the industry was moving from platforms to personalisation. With the advent of AI, we have to take it one step further. We have to ask what personalisation looks like when software stops waiting for humans to click and starts acting on intent.

Traditional banks did not lose control to fintechs. Regulation was stacked in their favour. If anything, they lost control of distribution.

The platform era taught the industry a brutal lesson: whoever owns the interface owns the context, the frequency, and the narrative. Banks retained balance sheets, but platforms controlled attention.

That dynamic was visible long before AI. Apple Pay did not replace banks, but it placed itself between the customer and the payment decision. Amazon did not become a bank, but it mastered intent at the moment of purchase. Tencent and Alibaba did not need banking licences to shape financial behaviour at scale.

Platforms understood something banks underestimated: personalisation is not a feature. It is a control system. It determines what the customer sees, when they see it, and what action feels natural next.

Now the control system is mutating again, because the interface itself is being unbundled. For two decades, software companies bundled three things into a single product: data, business logic, and interface. The interface was the moat. It trained user behaviour. It created switching costs. It held the relationship.

That moat is dissolving.

With protocols such as the Model Context Protocol[14], tools no longer need to be "opened" to be used. They can be invoked. And with the arrival of MCP Apps (the extension that allows tools to return interactive components), the interface can be rendered inside the conversational layer rather than inside the application itself. In practical terms, a task can move from "log into the tool, navigate the dashboard, export the file" to "tell the agent what you want and approve the action".

This changes the geography of power. The destination app becomes a backend. The relationship moves to the orchestration layer. And once the orchestration layer becomes the place where work happens, software stops being a set of products and becomes a set of callable capabilities.

In the platform era, personalisation was driven by feeds and recommendations. In the AI era, personalisation is driven by action.

This is where agents enter the story. An app waits for the user to act. An agent acts.

Agents observe signals, form beliefs, make decisions, and increasingly execute them. They represent customers, relationship managers, treasury desks, risk functions, and sometimes the institution itself. They do not sit neatly inside product silos or reporting lines.

This is why agents are not a feature.

They are an organisational unit.

And they introduce a new form of competition: not between apps, but between operating models. The winning institution will be the one that can govern agents, not merely deploy them.

## Generative AI and the Customer's Narrative

Generative AI changes the customer's role in banking before it changes the bank's systems.

For the first time, customers are not merely selecting from products or responding to offers. They are generating narratives: descriptions of intent, explanations of need, projections of future behaviour, and even draft financial structures expressed in natural language.

A customer no longer asks, "What products do you have?" They say, "Here is my situation. This is what I am trying to achieve. This are the risks I am willing to accept."

Generative models translate that narrative into structured intent. They produce scenarios, cash-flow projections, investment theses, hedging rationales, and even proto-contracts. In doing so, they invert the traditional product hierarchy.

This matters because banks have historically controlled finance by controlling the vocabulary. Products were defined in institutional language. Risk was described in internal terms. Customers adapted themselves to the bank's grammar. Generative AI breaks that asymmetry.

Customers now arrive with machine-generated coherence. Their narratives are internally consistent, analytically framed, and emotionally persuasive. They can articulate credit rationales and liquidity needs in ways that previously required a relationship manager.

This does not mean customers become their own banks. It means meaning shifts upstream. The bank no longer owns the first draft of intent. It receives it.

And once intent is expressed in machine-readable form, it becomes executable.

This is where generative AI meets agentic AI. Generative systems create the story. Agentic systems act on it.

## Web3 Is Not Web 3.0

This is also why the distinction between Web3 and Web 3.0 matters far more than the labels suggest.

The early internet promised decentralisation.

What it delivered was concentration.

Markets learned how to exploit networks faster than states learned how to regulate them. In the Web 3.0 version of the internet, platforms emerged as new market-makers, extracting rents from attention, data, and distribution. Banks were not displaced, but they were hollowed out. They retained assets and liabilities while losing narrative control.

Web3 is the permissionless world: blockchains, DeFi, tokens, composable money that is trying to bring back the decentralisation. Financial logic expressed directly in code, running continuously. I call it the world that Gavin Wood, the co-founder of Ethereum, created.

Web 3.0 is the semantic world: meaning layered over content, often centralised, often platform-controlled. This is the http world created by Tim Berners-Lee. It reinforces centralisation.

The two are in a tight fight to define what platforms really should be, personalised in a way that blockchain allows them to be, or public as the world wide web is today.

Banks are caught between these worlds, but they think its semantics.

Web3 challenges the bank's monopoly on settlement and custody.

Web 3.0 challenges the bank's monopoly on interpretation and distribution.

Add the Internet of Things, embedded sensors, and always-on context, and the bank's interface becomes ambient. The customer's financial life is no longer episodic. It is continuous.

This is how platforms become agents. If these agents sit on traditional platforms, the bank will control the relationship. If these agents sit in blockchain based systems, the customer will control the relationships and the networks and communities around them.

The strategic question for the AI Bank is not, "how do we build better apps?"

It is, "How do we remain the institution that retains the power of the relationship?"

Where platforms mediated access, AI mediates decision-making itself. When intelligence sits between signal and execution, speed compounds asymmetrically. Advantage accrues to institutions that sense earlier, decide faster, and act continuously.

## Why AI, CeFi, DeFi, and TradFi Must Be Read Together

At moments of structural change, leaders often try to simplify the story by separating worlds. Artificial intelligence is discussed in one conversation. Crypto in another. Traditional banking in a third.

That separation is no longer defensible.

AI will not be delivered to financial services exclusively through regulated institutions, nor will it respect the boundaries between centralised and decentralised systems. It is being deployed through networks, protocols, and orchestration layers that cut across institutional categories. The unit of change is no longer the product or the platform, but the workflow.

Decentralised finance matters in this context not because it will replace banks, a claim that has always been exaggerated, but because it has demonstrated what programmable settlement looks like at scale. Public blockchains have shown that assets, collateral, and liquidity can move automatically, atomically, and transparently under predefined rules. Whatever their volatility or governance challenges, these systems proved that settlement can be composable.

Centralised finance contributes something equally critical: balance sheets, supervision, customer recourse, and the capacity to absorb loss. When markets fail, when fraud occurs, when liquidity evaporates, it is regulated institutions that are called upon to stabilise the system. That role does not disappear simply because execution becomes automated.

Traditional finance provides the final anchor: clearing, legal finality, enforceable contracts, and the rule of law. Even the most technologically advanced markets ultimately depend on courts, custodians, and central banks to resolve disputes and confer legitimacy.

These are not competing ideologies. They are becoming a stack.

What changes is how the stack is coordinated.

AI now sits above these layers as a decision and orchestration engine. It does not replace balance sheets, blockchains, or clearing systems. It routes between them. It evaluates options, reprices risk, shifts collateral, arbitrages across rails, and increasingly initiates execution. Early forms of this already exist in algorithmic trading, automated treasury, and real-time fraud systems. The difference now is autonomy and scope.

This is where the model becomes an operator rather than an assistant.

Models are no longer designed merely to answer questions or summarise documents. They are being structured to ingest entire contexts, perform multi-step reasoning, interact with tools, and carry tasks through to completion under supervision. In finance, that means reading filings, building models, stress-testing assumptions, producing analysis, and preparing execution paths in a single workflow.

The implication is uncomfortable but unavoidable.

Banks will increasingly be asked to provide regulated execution, custody, and trust into flows they do not fully originate or control. Decisions will be shaped upstream by agents operating across centralised and decentralised rails, optimising for outcomes humans cannot see in real time.

In this environment, survival will not favour the institution that shouts "permissioned" the loudest or defends its perimeter most aggressively. It will favour the institution that can bridge CeFi, DeFi, and TradFi while preserving governance, accountability, and trust.

The AI Bank is not built by choosing sides.
It is built by learning how to operate coherently across all of them.

# CHAPTER TWO

# Where is AI Taking Us?

*"We are in the mainframe days of AI."*
*– Jayshree Ullal, CEO of Arista*[15]

---

This quote from Jayshree Ullal, the CEO of Arista, a company that is the physical backbone of the modern internet that few have even heard of, puts us in perspective[16]. Arista builds the high-performance networking infrastructure that hyperscalers, data centres, and AI workloads depend on. Ullal creates the highways on which Nvidia chips are able to run at speed she enables[17]. Her perspective is shaped by congestion, latency, and architectural stress, not by product demos or venture narratives.

Her bias is infrastructure realism.

When AI demand surges, she sees it not as excitement, but as pressure on networks, compute, and power. From that vantage point, her observation is not that AI is immature, but that it is centralised, brittle, and expensive, in exactly the way early mainframes were.

Compute is concentrated.
Models are large.
Access is mediated.
Control mechanisms lag execution.

Institutions bend themselves around the AI machine because the machine is rare, powerful, and difficult to govern.

This is exactly how the mainframe era felt inside banks. It's capability was impressive, but fragile. Governance lagged technology. Organisations structured themselves around technical constraints rather than institutional intent.

AI is doing the same thing today.

When I ask senior banking executives where they think AI is taking their institutions, the answers usually cluster around familiar themes.

Some talk about productivity. Faster onboarding. Better customer service. Lower cost-to-serve. Copilots for relationship managers and analysts. These answers are not wrong, but they are incomplete. They describe improvements in how work is done, not changes in how decisions are formed and executed.

Others hesitate. They talk about speed, uncertainty, and a vague sense that control is slipping. They struggle to articulate exactly what is changing, but they feel that something structural is moving underneath the institution.

That hesitation is the more important signal.

Boards approve models because they are scarce and powerful. Business units queue behind central AI teams. Risk and compliance slow decision cycles because they can see, correctly, that decision velocity has outpaced governance velocity.

This phase will not last. But it explains why so many banks feel simultaneously excited and uneasy.

## Decentralising Intelligence

AI will not remain centralised, dominated by a few players, as it appears to be heading today.

This is not because frontier models stop mattering, but because economics, regulation, and operational reality force intelligence closer to where decisions are made.

You can already see this in how the AI industry talks about its own future.

At Nvidia, Jensen Huang has repeatedly described a world in which training remains centralised, but inference moves outward, into factories, vehicles, robots, and devices[18]. His bias is shaped by physics: latency, energy consumption, and resilience make it impossible to route every decision through a handful of cloud data centres.

It is also shaped by the economics of capital infrastructure. It cannot be monolithic for too long.

In pharmaceuticals, the lesson is even clearer.

The pharmaceutical giant Moderna is often described as an "AI company," but that framing misses the point. Moderna is AI-native because it embedded machine intelligence across the entire decision loop: drug discovery, trial design, manufacturing scale-up, and supply-chain optimisation. Models operate under regulatory constraint, with traceability and intervention designed in from the start.

Accuracy matters. Control matters more.

This is not yet a banking story. It is a systems story. But banking always follows systems once scale and risk collide.

What emerges is a recognisable trajectory:

- Models become smaller and more specialised.
- Inference moves closer to execution.
- Institutions insist on sovereignty over models and data.
- Systems reason across text, images, behaviour, and sensor signals.
- And, crucially, systems stop advising and start acting.

That last step is the inflection point that I will expand in the rest of the book.

## When the User Defines the Context

One of the least discussed but most consequential developments in the AI ecosystem is the rise of Model Context Protocols (MCP)[19].

MCP is not a model innovation. It is an access innovation.

For the first time, end users can define what context an AI system sees, how it is refreshed, and how it is acted upon without waiting for an institution to redesign its interface. Context becomes something you can plug in, swap out, audit, and govern.

At first glance, that sounds mundane. Of course software should connect to other software. But in banking, the ability to define context is the ability to define reality. It determines what the agent "knows", what it can retrieve, what it can call, and what it can change.

In the old world, the interface was the gatekeeper. If a workflow was not in the menu, it did not exist. If a data field was not in the dashboard, it was operationally invisible. MCP shifts that power away from the application layer and toward the orchestration layer.

Then the story accelerated.

MCP Apps added a new dimension: not just returning data to a chat window, but returning interactive user interface components. In other words, the tool can ship its interface into the agent. A task board, a chart, a form, a slider, a dashboard. The user can act without leaving the conversation. The workflow becomes continuous rather than tabbed.

This is not simply convenience. It is a transfer of relationship. If the user interacts with Asana or Figma or analytics tools through the agent's interface, the agent becomes the daily workplace and the underlying applications become interchangeable infrastructure.

This is the deeper implication for financial services. Banks have historically controlled customer journeys by controlling channels. But the channel is now a negotiable layer. When the interface becomes portable, banks cannot rely on "our app" or "our portal" as the primary place where decisions are made. They have to compete to be the most trusted execution environment inside someone else's orchestration layer.

That is why the governance of MCP matters. When a protocol moves from vendor feature to neutral infrastructure, it becomes harder to ignore and harder to fight. With MCP being placed under a foundation model for industry stewardship, it has begun to take the shape of a standard rather than a product. Standards do not need to be perfect to win. They just need enough adoption to become inevitable.

In that world, the competitive question becomes simple and uncomfortable: if customers define the context and agents define the workflow, what exactly does the bank still control?

## The Shift from Language to Action

Much of today's AI discussion still centres on generative AI: systems that produce text, images, code, and explanations. These systems matter because they change *meaning*.

Generative AI reshapes how intent is expressed.

Customers arrive with machine-generated narratives: structured explanations of needs, risks, preferences, and future plans. Analysts receive drafts that already embed assumptions. Regulators receive reports that are internally coherent before a human edits them.

Meaning moves upstream.

Some of the most influential figures shaping this layer come from outside banking.

Sam Altman, the founder of OpenAI the company that runs ChatGPT, has consistently framed large language models as general-purpose reasoning systems rather than narrow tools[20]. His bias is scale: once language becomes programmable, coordination costs collapse.

Demis Hassabis, coming from a scientific background, and focused on Artificial General Intelligence, emphasises systems that learn, plan, and act across domains. His focus is not productivity, but generalised problem-solving under constraint[21].

But generative AI is only half the story.

The more consequential shift is toward agentic AI: systems that do not just generate outputs, but pursue goals, make decisions, and execute actions across time.

Here, voices like Yoshua Bengio matter enormously. Bengio's concern is not interface risk, but emergent behaviour in multi-agent, networked systems[22]. His bias is structural: once agents optimise simultaneously inside shared environments, behaviour can align and cascade faster than humans can intervene.

In practice, this means:

- Generative AI shapes belief.
- Agentic AI turns belief into action.

Once those two layers combine, the focus shifts to governance.

## Ambient Finance and the End of the Device

By device, I simply mean the ubiquitous mobile device we are all dependent on today.

Mobile banking felt transformative because it changed *where* banking happened. It did not change *how* banking decided. AI will.

Finance followed humans onto screens because screens were where attention lived. AI breaks that logic. Intelligence does not require attention. It requires context.

This is where the Internet of Things (IoT) enters the picture.

Household appliances, vehicles, industrial machines, and energy systems are becoming sensor-rich, networked, and decision-capable. Refrigerators know consumption patterns. Electric vehicles know charging behaviour. Home energy systems know load, pricing, and grid stress. Insurance-linked sensors know risk before a claim exists.

In this environment, finance becomes ambient.

A household appliance does not "log into" a bank. It negotiates energy usage, maintenance schedules, and insurance coverage continuously. Credit and payment decisions are embedded into usage patterns, not triggered by applications.

You can already see this outside banking.

At Tesla, financial decisions are embedded directly into the vehicle: charging optimisation, insurance pricing, maintenance risk, and usage-based cost allocation occur continuously, without a banking interface ever opening.

In supply-chain finance, IoT sensors link inventory levels, temperature, location, and transit risk directly to credit availability. Liquidity appears when conditions demand it, not when a form is submitted.

In emerging markets, this logic arrives faster. Where formal financial touchpoints are scarce, finance becomes ambient by necessity, not by design.

This is why the AI Bank is not about better apps. It marks the end of the interface as the primary control surface.

## Navigating the Path of Least Resistance

Intelligence always routes toward environments where execution is cheapest and cleanest.

When systems encounter friction, they route around it. This is not ideology. It is operational logic.

This explains why AI gravitates toward environments where rules are machine-readable, execution is automated, and settlement is final. It also explains why early AI-driven financial experimentation often appears outside traditional banking perimeters.

Banks that cannot match this execution certainty are not displaced overnight.

They are bypassed incrementally.

The pressure does not land first on customer experience.

It lands on the balance sheet, because when intelligence moves at machine speed, the first constraint it collides with is not technology.

It is funding, liquidity, and trust.

This chapter is not a forecast. It is a map. AI is moving:

- from centre to edge
- from language to action
- from interface to environment
- from episodic decisions to continuous execution

Banks that recognise this trajectory early can redesign deliberately.

Banks that do not will discover it only when behaviour escapes control and remediation arrives too late.

That is why the next chapter turns to the balance sheet itself and how it is an integral part of the ecosystem that has to be redefined for the AI age.

# CHAPTER THREE

# Building the AI Operating Model

*"We shape our tools and thereafter our tools shape us."*
*– Marshall McLuhan*[23]

I meet with boards where progress is still narrated through familiar numbers. How many pilots are running. How many use cases are live. How many processes have been automated. How many announcements can be cited as evidence that the institution is "doing AI."

Most banks are measuring the wrong thing.
And most of the people in the room already know it.

The numbers accumulate quickly. They look disciplined. They travel well in slides. But they say very little about whether the bank is actually becoming an AI bank.

This is where Fei-Fei Li's critique of runaway AI hype lands uncomfortably close to home for banking. Speaking publicly at the World Economic Forum and elsewhere, she has warned against mistaking demonstrations for impact, arguing that institutions too often celebrate what is technically impressive while failing to measure what is economically and socially meaningful[24].

Banks today are drowning in pilots that generate activity but not institutional progress.

In the digital banking era, a pilot proved that a feature could be shipped. It showed that a team could build something new, integrate it into existing systems, and deploy it without breaking the institution. That was a real achievement.

In the AI banking era, a pilot must prove something far more uncomfortable. It must show that judgement itself can be embedded into systems, supervised continuously, corrected when it fails, and stopped when it becomes dangerous, all without destabilising the institution.

That distinction is easy to underestimate, particularly for leaders who successfully lived through digital transformation and assume this is simply the next chapter of the same journey.

It is not.

Once judgement moves into machines, measuring uplift alone becomes dangerously insufficient. Banks have to learn to measure failure, not philosophically, but operationally. Bias variance. Override integrity. Incident frequency. Drift detection. Recoverability. Customer harm avoided.

A pilot that cannot be observed, governed, and shut down safely is not really a pilot at all. It is a demonstration. And demonstrations are cheap. Institutions are not.

So the real question is not whether intelligence is being deployed. It is whether intelligence is being embedded safely, continuously, and with measurable impact on institutional resilience.

A good AI bank is not defined by how many tools it deploys. It is defined by whether it can govern judgement.

## Who owns the decisions?

This is where many banks slip into a familiar comfort zone.

From the perspective of platform providers, the story makes sense. Executives talk about infrastructure readiness, deployment capability, and repeatable implementation patterns. Banks need that practicality. They need tooling. They need scale. They need models they can run.

But tooling is not transformation.

AI forces organisations to re-examine how decisions are actually made, not just how systems are run. It collapses the gap between analysis and action. It compresses the time between signal and execution. It increases the number of decisions made per hour and reduces the number of humans present when those decisions are made.

That is not a technology problem. It is a governance problem.

The practical question is this: when a model proposes a credit limit change, reprices a portfolio, flags a transaction, or routes a payment, who owns that decision? Who is accountable for the outcome? And who can prove, under pressure, why that decision was made?

Banks cannot answer these questions with organisational charts. They need decision rights that are explicit at machine speed.

This becomes sharper as AI moves from "assistant" to "operator".

The clearest signal of that shift is that the models are being designed to operate inside real tasks, not just produce text. Anthropic's Claude Opus 4.6 is framed less as a smarter chatbot and more as a model capable of multi-step knowledge workflows: ingesting long documents, working across spreadsheets, producing structured analysis and presentations, and chaining actions inside supervised agent loops[25]. This is not speculative. It is the direction of product design.

And as models become operators, a second question becomes existential: who owns the state?

If the model vendor owns the workflow state, the memory, the tool permissions, and the audit trail, the bank becomes locked into the vendor's operating system for decision-making. Switching models becomes expensive not because the model is unique, but because the institution's decision context is trapped.

If the bank owns the state, the model becomes a replaceable component. The bank can treat models as competing engines rather than as sovereign platforms. It can swap models, use multiple models, and shift workloads without surrendering governance.

This is not a philosophical debate. It is a strategic design choice.

Banks have always been regulated not because they hold data, but because they execute decisions with real-world consequences. In the AI era, the institution that survives is the one that can make decision ownership legible even when the decision itself is generated, routed, and partially executed by agents.

## Measuring the right matrix

When boards ask what an AI operating model actually consists of, they are rarely asking for another diagram. What they want to know is whether the institution will still hold together when decisions start happening faster than people can convene.

This is why the operating model resolves into a small set of non-negotiable capabilities.

Data and infrastructure are not about ever-larger data lakes. They are about readiness. Lineage that can be explained under pressure. Integration that does not fracture when new models are introduced. Compute sufficiency that does not force trade-offs between speed and control. And context design that is intentional, not accidental.

If your institution cannot define, refresh, and audit what the model sees, it cannot govern what the model does.

Governance and risk are not ethics committees. They show up in active board oversight, in model inventories that are current rather than retrospective, in explainability evidence that exists before incidents, not after, and in override mechanisms that actually work. The operating model must assume that AI will sometimes be wrong in ways that look plausible. Governance must be built for plausible error, not obvious failure.

Execution is not a downstream detail. It is the boundary where responsibility becomes real. The moment the model can initiate actions, not just recommendations, the bank must have control points that are designed into the workflow: approvals, thresholds, dual control, and audit trails that capture not only the final action but the context that produced it.

This is also why "pilot counting" is the wrong metric. The more pilots, the better.

In 2026, the model is increasingly becoming the interface. And once the interface is mediated by an agent, capability compounds. A small improvement in tool-use reliability can eliminate entire layers of manual checking, spreadsheet stitching, and report assembly. The time saved is not just productivity. It is a reallocation of institutional attention. Less time gathering. Less time formatting. More time interrogating assumptions and defending judgments.

The bar for entry-level execution drops. The bar for judgment rises.

So the right metrics are not "how many AI projects do we have?" They are: how many critical decisions have machine-speed governance? How many workflows have explicit decision rights? How often can we reconstruct what the model saw, what it called, what it proposed, and why we approved it? How quickly can we switch models without losing state?

If the board cannot answer those questions, it does not yet have an AI operating model.

## A Note to Digital-Only Banks

There is a separate conversation that needs to be had explicitly, and it is often the most uncomfortable one.

Digital-only banks did many things right. They rebuilt distribution. They modernised stacks. They reduced cost-to-serve. They proved that customers would move money when friction disappeared.

In doing so, they forced incumbents to move faster than they wanted to.

But in most cases, they did not redesign judgement.

Credit decisions remained episodic. Liquidity was still managed in batches. Fraud controls were reactive. Products were static. Information was treated as exhaust rather than as a live decision asset.

The architecture changed. The logic did not.

Anne Boden, founder of Starling Bank, has written candidly about how difficult it is to move from modern interfaces to genuinely adaptive decision-making once scale is reached[26]. Her point is not that digital banks failed technologically, but that judgement is harder to modernise than distribution.

AI is unforgiving to that gap.

For digital-only banks, the strategic question is not how to add generative AI features. It is what the digital bank was actually for. If the answer was cheaper acquisition and better experience, AI will commoditise that advantage. If the answer was owning decision intelligence, AI becomes an accelerant.

Digital-only banks still retain one advantage incumbents often lack: architectural freedom. Whether it matters now depends entirely on whether that freedom is used to redesign decision surfaces rather than automate workflows.

## Execution Beyond the Institution

Even a perfectly governed institution can still lose relevance.

Digital banking trained banks to compete for attention. AI banking forces them to compete for execution.

When customers bring their own agents, distribution is no longer an app or a branch. Selection happens inside interactions between systems.

This is where BNY Mellon's internal framing, articulated publicly by Sarthak Pattanaik, its chief data and AI officer, becomes instructive[27]. "AI for everyone, everywhere, in everything" captures the reality that agentic capability becomes ambient across workflows. The unspoken qualifier is governance. Without it, scale simply multiplies error.

Institutions are no longer chosen because they are familiar. They are chosen because their behaviour is legible, predictable, and reliable under stress.

This reframes partnerships entirely.

Many banks still talk about partnerships as if they were in the API era. In the digital age, partnerships meant access. The bank provided accounts and compliance. The partner provided engagement.

AI breaks this model.

Speaking on fintech panels, Jackie Reses, chairwoman and CEO of Lead Bank in Kansas, has described how software companies increasingly selects partners based on execution reliability rather than brand or relationship. In an agent-mediated environment, institutions are routed around not because they are untrusted, but because they are unpredictable[28].

In an AI world, partnerships are about shared execution surfaces. Whether agents can act across institutional boundaries. Whether data and liquidity flow with consent. Whether control rules are mutually legible.

Banks that insist on owning the interface will fade quietly. Banks that insist on owning decision constraints and execution rights will remain central.

Partnerships determine where the bank can show up.
Products determine what the bank becomes.

# CHAPTER FOUR

# The Balance Sheet Comes to Life

*"Facts do not cease to exist because they are ignored."*
*– Aldous Huxley*[29]

---

In building the operating mode of the bank, let's go back to the core of the business.

It will be tempting to think that the balance sheet will no longer be the business in an AI world. This temptation already appeared in the digital banking era, when technologists came to the fore and made it look as if the interfaces were the business. They were so wrong.

The balance sheet remains the core of banking. It is where risk is carried, where confidence is underwritten, and where failure ultimately crystallises. What has changed is not its importance, but how it behaves and where control over it now resides.

In the AI Bank, balance-sheet strength without decision intelligence becomes utility finance. You warehouse risk. Someone else intermediates intent. Someone else captures the economics.

The balance sheet is still the business. It is no longer the control surface.

For most of modern banking history, balance sheets were governed as static objects.

Assets were originated, booked, and held. Liabilities were assumed to be sticky. Risk was measured periodically. Liquidity stress was modelled as a scenario, not experienced as a continuous condition. Committees reviewed outcomes after the fact. Intervention followed reports.

Digital banking did not fundamentally change this.
It accelerated access, not behaviour.

The collapse of Silicon Valley Bank should be read less as a story about asset quality and more as a story about velocity.

SVB did not fail because its assets were uniquely toxic. It failed because information moved faster than governance. Depositors did not read financial statements. They reacted to belief propagated through digital channels. Liquidity evaporated in days. Committees convened too slowly. By the time humans intervened, the system had already decided.

The notion of "sticky" or "lazy" deposits is already a historical anomaly. But banks still offer near-to-nothing interest in their time deposits that some rich depositors sit in their accounts and it appears to be okay.

AI-enabled digital wallets will increasingly sweep idle balances automatically into the highest-yielding, lowest-friction instruments available — whether money-market funds, tokenised treasuries, or alternative settlement systems. The implication is stark: deposit inertia was a feature of low information velocity, not a permanent banking advantage.

When information, belief, and execution align at machine speed, the balance sheet stops behaving like an accounting object and starts behaving like a live, breathing organism.

## AI as a Balance-Sheet Amplifier

Artificial intelligence does not introduce new categories of balance-sheet risk.
It amplifies existing ones.

Better prediction alters liquidity needs. Faster sensing reshapes capital buffers. Automated decision-making scales exposure at machine speed. Correlated models respond simultaneously to the same signals.

This is not theoretical.

At JPMorgan Chase, executives have spoken publicly about using AI to compress stress-testing cycles and detect behavioural shifts earlier[30]. The emphasis is not on improving forecast accuracy by a few basis points. It is on reducing the time between signal and intervention.

This framing reflects a very specific institutional bias. JPMorgan's challenge is not whether it can absorb losses. It is whether it can see behaviour early enough to prevent cascades.

In emerging markets, the dynamic is even more immediate.

Many bank balance sheets are already being repriced by the market as *stranded.* Duration mismatch is a normal, accepted feature of the balance sheet today In an AI Bank, there will be not only a duration mismatch, but the structural exposure to commercial real estate, legacy auto loans, and branch-based cost structures will just not adapt at the speed AI-mediated finance demands. Banks will not be undercapitalized; but increasingly overexposed to assets whose very economic logic is disappearing.

## Treasury in a Game of Thrones

When leaders talk about the Treasury function in a bank abstractly, they miss how physical and immediate the job actually is.

In most banks, Treasury's day begins before the rest of the organisation logs on. Not with a meeting, but with screens. Intraday liquidity positions. Settlement obligations. Collateral movements. Funding capacity by entity, by currency, by counterparty. The question is never *"what will the balance sheet look like this quarter?"* It is *"what could break before lunch?"*

That framing is no longer anecdotal. Senior executives responsible for liquidity at the largest institutions have been explicit that intraday visibility and real-time funding control are now operating requirements, not planning luxuries. When JPMorgan Chase's Jennifer Piepszak has spoken publicly about liquidity management, her emphasis has consistently been on *operability*: the ability to see, act, and intervene continuously[31]. The implication is unspoken but clear. Treasury no longer controls the clock. It reacts to it.

A modern Treasury function therefore operates through three overlapping loops, whether it explicitly names them or not.

The first is the intraday liquidity loop. Payments move. Margin calls land. Large corporate sweeps hit accounts. Clearing and settlement obligations spike unexpectedly. Treasury has minutes, sometimes seconds, to decide whether to fund, throttle, reroute, or absorb. AI is useful here only insofar as it improves visibility and prioritisation. By the time a report confirms stress, it is already too late.

This is precisely the dynamic regulators have been warning about. When Agustín Carstens, then the General Manager of the BIS, spoke about automation and market speed, his concern was not technology risk in isolation, but procyclicality. When liquidity responds at machine speed, it ceases to be a buffer and becomes an amplifier. Treasury stops smoothing cycles and starts firefighting them.

The second is the behavioural loop. Retail deposits are treated as stable funding right up until the moment they behave like information products. Treasury watches concentrations, rate-sensitive segments, digital-only cohorts, and "hot money" patterns. AI matters here not as prediction theatre, but as early warning and segmentation.

This is where the traditional idea of a "sticky" deposit base quietly collapses. Central bankers like Andrew Bailey, governor of the Bank of England, have repeatedly pointed out that non-bank financial intermediation and market-based finance have eroded banks' ability to dampen liquidity shocks[32]. From a Treasury perspective, that means funding behaviour is increasingly shaped outside the institution. Deposits move not because pricing changes, but because confidence does.

The third is the market loop. Swap spreads, basis moves, collateral haircuts, repo availability, and microstructure volatility all translate directly into funding reality. Treasury's role is to convert market signals into institutional constraints: *we can price like this, we must slow that, we need term funding today.*

Academic work makes clear why this loop no longer behaves the way ALM models assume. Hyun Song Shin, now Chief Economist at the BIS, has shown that modern liquidity is endogenous. It is created by balance-sheet behaviour, collateral reuse, and market confidence — and withdrawn just as quickly when behaviour turns. Cost of funds is no longer a stable internal parameter. It is a moving target shaped by the system itself.

So far, this still sounds like an intensified version of a job Treasury has always done.

The deeper shift comes next.

In an AI economy, Treasury is no longer arbitrating only between internal balance-sheet constraints and market prices. It is arbitrating against a continuously repricing external system, where the cost of funds, the availability of assets, and the routes through which liquidity can flow are themselves in motion.

Historically, banks were privileged arbitrators of liquidity. Deposits were sticky. Funding markets moved in recognisable cycles. Asset availability was mediated through institutional channels. The bank's internal cost of funds was the primary reference point.

That assumption breaks when capital markets reprice continuously, collateral is mobilised and rehypothecated across venues at machine speed, and non-bank balance sheets offer alternative liquidity paths in real time. As Stanford finance professor Darrell Duffie has argued, market-based liquidity increasingly substitutes for bank balance-sheet intermediation. Treasury no longer sets the menu[33]. It competes inside it.

This is why cost of funds becomes contextual, not averaged.

A customer's agent does not care what the bank's internal FTP says. It cares whether liquidity is available now, at what price, with what certainty, and with what recourse. If an alternative route exists through a market rail, a tokenised instrument, or a non-bank intermediary, the agent will discover it — and that discovery feeds back into Treasury's reality.

The same applies on the asset side. In an AI economy, the range of assets available for funding, collateralisation, or risk transfer expands and contracts continuously. Tokenised deposits, digitised securities, repo instruments, and synthetic exposures move faster than traditional ALM assumptions allow. Assets no longer wait to be acted upon. They signal intent. They attract or repel liquidity.

Treasury must therefore think not just in terms of what assets the bank holds, but what assets the market is offering as substitutes at any given moment. This is a profound shift.

The bank is no longer setting the clock.
It is negotiating relevance inside it.

This is why the AI Bank changes the Treasury job fundamentally.

The distance between market signal, decision, and execution collapses. Treasury stops being a reporting function and becomes a live intervention function. Authority moves from explanation to interruption.

It removes the illusion that cost of funds is stable.
That deposits are inert.
That assets wait.
That the bank controls timing.

In an AI economy, the clock belongs to execution.

Treasury does not lose power in this world.
But it loses exclusivity. It has to be grounded in a much larger narrative.

And leadership must decide whether the bank will compete as a passive provider of regulated liquidity — or as an active governor of when and how liquidity is allowed to move.

That choice is not made in a funding plan.

It is made in how Treasury is authorised to intervene — and when it is allowed to say no.

## When Treasury Goes Real-Time

What's striking is how rarely Treasury voices speak loudly about these shifts in public.

Liquidity is one of the few areas where narrative itself can move markets. Treasurers learn early that what they say externally can become behaviour internally.

So the signals appear indirectly.

When transaction banks like HSBC speak about "real-time treasury"[34] and AI-enabled cash management, the useful detail is not in the marketing language. It is the operating assumption underneath: treasury clients now expect decisions to be faster and more contextual. That expectation forces banks to upgrade how they sense, decide, and intervene.

Similarly, Citigroup has published research on generative AI in treasury that emphasises data foundations and incremental control rather than a grand transformation[35]. That emphasis is revealing. Treasury is becoming AI-native even as you read these pages.

None of this is yet the full AI Bank.
But it shows the direction of travel.

## The Retail–Treasury FTP Tension

This is also where the internal politics of the bank surface most clearly.

In the digital era, a head of retail could treat deposit pricing as a growth lever and let Treasury "fund it". Treasury would complain, but behaviour moves slowly enough for there to be a compromise. Everyone has time to argue, smooth out each other, and adjust.

That luxury disappears in the AI Bank.

What we need to imagine is not a quarterly negotiation, but a continuous one.

Retail wants growth, engagement, and retention. Treasury wants funding quality, predictability, and resilience. The tension is not ideological. It is operational.

Retail asks for real-time features. The question that treasury needs to ask is where the kill switches are.

In practice, the negotiation shifts away from headline price and toward constraints. Treasury increasingly defines the envelope within which Retail is allowed to optimise:

- Which customer segments can be targeted.
- Where rate changes must be throttled.
- What real-time withdrawal limits activate under stress.
- How deposits are classified for internal liquidity assumptions.

This is also where Funds Transfer Pricing stops being a back-office calculation and becomes a governance interface. Retail does not merely "receive FTP". It negotiates against a live cost-of-funds signal whose purpose is prudential, not commercial.

If I want to know whether a bank is genuinely becoming an AI Bank, I don't look at its chatbot. I sit in on this conversation. The frequency and intensity of the Retail–Treasury negotiation tells you everything about where control really sits.

In the digital era, FTP could lag reality. Funding costs were averaged. Pricing reflected yesterday's conditions. The system tolerated delay because customers moved slowly. The exercise is in itself static and hypothetical.

In the AI Bank, that tolerance disappears.

When customer agents and corporate treasuries arbitrage pricing in real time, FTP becomes a live signal, feeding directly into:

- product pricing
- credit limits
- liquidity routing
- execution throttles
- governance

This does not mean pricing becomes volatile by default.
It means pricing has to become governed.

The institution must decide when pricing adapts automatically, when it freezes, and when humans intervene. Most importantly, the pricing can be used by algorithms to respond to customer needs in a specific transaction in an instant.

Treasury's job is no longer to set prices alone. Its job is to design constraints within which the business can use dynamically to close sales that previously was impossible.

## Digital Assets on the Balance Sheet

Every bank in the world is discussing the day when digital assets will sit on the balance sheet. Most have no clue what it will mean.

The regulatory conversation is not about whether banks should "like" crypto. It will happen. But the thinking is coming from a world that is ceasing to exist like the smile on a Cheshire cat.

The Basel Committee on Banking Supervision has already published a detailed framework on the prudential treatment of banks' cryptoasset exposures.

The focus is explicit: prevent banks from importing unbounded volatility into the core system without recognising it in capital, liquidity, and disclosure.

Once digital assets appear on a bank's balance sheet, three things change immediately.

- Valuation becomes continuous, because the asset never sleeps.
- Liquidity assumptions fragment across venues and rails.
- Correlation risk becomes behavioural rather than statistical.

AI accentuates all these parameters. As I say elsewhere in this book, digital assets are AI -repositories. They can either weaponize or productize the balance sheet.

## Programmable Liabilities and Active Stability

The idea of programmable liabilities are already being tested in various jurisdictions today. But it is still not yet clear if it will be based on CBDCs or tokenized deposits issued by the banks. The sentiment I get is that banks understand that this might be the future trend, but none have any clue how these will work out as a business model.

It is still early days, and it may never come into fruition as this trend might be overtaken by developments in stable coins. But tokenised deposits and institution-issued stablecoins are early attempts to align inference with execution.

For the moment, JP Morgan Chase's JPM Coin[36] is not a retail crypto experiment. It is an internal settlement mechanism designed to make liquidity legible to machine-mediated decisioning.

Similarly, Standard Chartered has positioned tokenised money as infrastructure for cross-border liquidity and trade finance[37]. From its vantage point, programmability is not novelty. It is a stabiliser in fragmented, volatile markets.

As an AI tool, it is easy to see how programmable liabilities can become a vehicle to carry both inferences and execution. If this technology does take off, it will add another customer behavioral layer to the instability of the balance sheet that has to be actively managed as discussed in the sections above.

## US State Banks Already Living This

In the United States, several state-chartered institutions have already lived through what happens when payments, liquidity, and digital assets collide at machine speed.

Customer Bank, under CEO Jay Sidhu, became deeply involved in digital-asset related transaction flows[38]. Whatever one thinks of the strategy, the learning was real. When regulatory pressure arrived, the bank was forced to rethink not just exposure, but how quickly behaviour could propagate through payment rails tied to digital assets.

Custodia Bank and Vantage Bank have spoken publicly about tokenised deposit experiments and blockchain-based settlement[39]. These are not yet mainstream models, and they are not risk-free. But they are early illustrations of what "programmable liabilities" actually look like in practice.

Overlay this with interpretive guidance from US regulators allowing certain crypto custody and stablecoin-related activities, and the direction becomes clear: the stance has shifted from "don't touch" to "touch, but with controls".

The question every bank will eventually face is not whether digital assets belong on the balance sheet. It is whether a balance sheet governed in batches can survive in an environment where settlement and belief are tested 24 hours a day.

The lesson of AI is not that balance sheets disappear.

It is that they can no longer be governed through quarterly reviews, static stress tests, or assumptions of depositor inertia.

Once intelligence moves at machine speed, balance sheets move with it. The balance sheet is still the business. But control now lives elsewhere.

That is why the next chapter turns to payments, where balance-sheet behaviour becomes visible, irreversible, and immediately consequential.

# CHAPTER FIVE

# Payments as AI in Motion

*"AI is the new electricity."*
*– Jansen Huang*[40]

---

If you want to understand how banking actually works, don't start with products, channels or strategy decks. Start with payments.

Payments are the bloodstream of the business. Loans can be debated. Wealth can be discretionary. Products can be redesigned. But payments have to be deterministic.

Payments is where confidence becomes action, where belief turns into movement, and where failure reveals itself immediately. Customers notice payment failures before they notice almost anything else. Regulators fear payment failures because they propagate faster than any other banking malfunction.

That is why structural change in banking always shows up in payments first.

In the AI Bank, this is no longer incidental.

Banks today depend on all the possible frictions inherent in traditional payments. Three to five day settlement times, fees, exchange rates, more fees. The friction of the old system is the revenue of the banks.

When settlement becomes instant, programmable, and transparent, the fees and frictions that once sustained intermediaries are no longer defensible. AI's primary economic effect is to remove that friction.

## From Messaging to Execution

For decades, global payments functioned because the world moved slowly enough for humans and institutions to intervene.

Banks exchanged messages. Value moved later. Exceptions were handled manually. Compliance was layered on after the fact. Cross-border payments took days, sometimes weeks. Friction was tolerated because there was no credible alternative and because human judgement could still catch up.

That tolerance no longer exists.

Programmable money, real-time settlement rails, and automated compliance will turn payments from a messaging problem into an execution problem. Value can now move conditionally, continuously, and with finality, without waiting for humans to reconcile intent after the fact.

Then when you add the fact that a lot of these payments will be made on stablecoins, cryptocurrencies and even tokenized deposits, you have to recognize they carry more than just messages.

As I described in my first book, payments carry identity, verification, value, and information (IVVI) together. In an AI-native payment process:

- **Identity** is persistent and portable, not account-information.
- **Verification** is continuous, not episodic.
- **Value** is programmable, not merely recorded.
- **Information** travels with the execution, not after it.

This IVVI convergence is what allows intelligence to act safely at speed. Remember, it is possible to have multiple identities with AI, so identity alone is insufficient to validate a transaction. It is also what makes payments such a critical control surface. When value moves, identity, verification, and information must move with it.

This is not a marginal efficiency gain.
It is a categorical shift.

From the perspective of AI, this shift is non-negotiable. Intelligence cannot operate on promises of value that arrive later. It requires settlement that is observable, controllable, and final at the moment of the decision.

Stress shows up in payments before it shows up anywhere else.

Credit quality deteriorates slowly. Capital ratios lag reality. Liquidity buffers buy time. But payments reveal behaviour in motion. They are where intent turns into action and where confidence becomes observable.

When depositors lose confidence, they do not debate. They move money.
When corporates sense uncertainty, they reroute liquidity.
When agents detect risk, they do not escalate to committees. They execute.

In an AI Bank, this dynamic becomes unavoidable. Once decisions are automated and behaviour accelerates, payments stop being the final step of a process and become the first place instability materializes.

This is why regulators, whether they articulate it explicitly or not, increasingly treat payment flows as early-warning systems for institutional stress.

## Cross-Border CBDC Pilots

Over the past few years, central banks have launched a series of cross-border CBDC and wholesale settlement pilots, often presented as technical proofs of concept. Read in isolation, these projects look like incremental improvements to correspondent banking. Read together, they reveal something more comical.

From a central bank perspective, the motivation is clear: faster settlement, lower cost, reduced correspondent risk. From an AI perspective, these systems still behave like messaging corridors.

They are permissioned, hub-and-spoke, and governance-heavy. They demonstrate that settlement can be faster, but not yet that it can be autonomous.

Expose these systems to AI-mediated flows at scale and friction appears immediately: governance bottlenecks, jurisdictional conflicts, and incentive misalignment.

They are attempts to restore observability and control over payment flows in a world that is moving faster than existing governance structures can tolerate.

One of the earliest and most cited experiments was Project Jasper–Ubin, a collaboration between the Bank of Canada[41] and the Monetary Authority of Singapore[42]. The project demonstrated that atomic, cross-border settlement using wholesale CBDCs was technically feasible. Value could move instantly and irreversibly across jurisdictions.

What Jasper–Ubin does not attempt to solve is behaviour under stress.

It assumed a small set of trusted participants, pre-agreed rules, and orderly execution. From a prudential perspective, it answered the question "can settlement be faster?" It did not answer "what happens when flows accelerate non-linearly and confidence breaks?"

France approached the problem through Project Jura, led by the Banque de France with the Swiss National Bank[43]. Jura focused on cross-border delivery-versus-payment between euro and Swiss franc CBDCs, explicitly prioritising legal finality and jurisdictional clarity.

That bias is important. Jura optimised for legal correctness, not adaptive behaviour. Execution was subordinated to governance. In an AI-mediated world, that trade-off becomes visible very quickly. AI systems do not wait for legal elegance. They optimise for certainty of execution.

The most ambitious multilateral effort to date has been Project Dunbar, coordinated by the BIS Innovation Hub, involving the central banks of Singapore, Australia, Malaysia, and South Africa. Project Dunbar explored a shared multi-CBDC platform where commercial banks could transact across currencies on a common ledger[44].

Project Dunbar is revealing because it exposes the real difficulty: governance does not scale linearly. Every additional central bank adds rule-sets, exceptions, and veto points. From an AI perspective, Dunbar still behaves like a negotiated corridor, not an executable fabric. Settlement is faster, but intervention remains slow.

The closest any project has come to production-like conditions is Project mBridge, involving the People's Bank of China, the Hong Kong Monetary Authority, the Bank of Thailand, and the Central Bank of the UAE[45]. mBridge operates a live, multi-currency platform for wholesale cross-border payments, particularly in trade settlement.

mBridge matters because it reflects a different institutional bias: scale first, governance later. It is the most operational of the pilots, but it remains permissioned, rule-driven, and centrally supervised. It has not yet been tested against autonomous, AI-driven routing under stress.

Europe's Project Helvetia, led by the Swiss National Bank with the BIS and SIX, took yet another approach[46]. Rather than redesign settlement, it sought to integrate wholesale CBDCs into existing financial market infrastructure. The bias here is continuity. Modernise without destabilising. Preserve stop-power by keeping execution close to existing control points.

Finally, Project Icebreaker, involving the central banks of Sweden, Norway, Israel, and the BIS, explored interoperability between domestic CBDC systems through a hub-and-spoke model[47]. Icebreaker demonstrated that interoperability is technically achievable. It also demonstrated that governance coordination, not technology, becomes the bottleneck almost immediately.

Seen through the lens of the AI Bank, these projects share a striking commonality.

They all prioritise sovereign observability.
They all assume human-paced governance.
They all embed explicit stop-power at the centre.

This is not accidental.

Central banks understand, even if they do not always say it publicly, that once payment flows become autonomous, the ability to *see* and *interrupt* behaviour matters more than the ability to *optimise* it.

This is also where observability stops being an operational concern and becomes a prudential requirement.

Traditional supervision assumed that behaviour could be reconstructed after the fact. Reports arrived later. Exceptions were investigated. Controls were audited periodically. That model depended on delay.

It breaks down when execution happens at machine speed.

In an AI Bank, the key question is no longer "did this transaction comply?"
It is "can we see behaviour as it unfolds, and can we intervene before it cascades?"

Observability here does not mean dashboards.

It means real-time visibility into flows, the ability to classify behaviour as it emerges, the authority to throttle, segment, or halt execution, and the capacity to explain decisions while they are happening, not days later.

From a prudential perspective, this is decisive. A bank that cannot observe its payment flows at machine speed is not conservative. It is blind.

What these pilots do not yet accommodate is AI-mediated behaviour at scale.

An AI-driven treasury system does not want to choose between two pre-approved corridors. It wants to route liquidity dynamically across multiple rails, currencies, and jurisdictions based on price, risk, and confidence signals. It wants to do this continuously, not episodically.

Expose these current CBDC pilots to that reality and three tensions appear immediately.

First, observability gaps emerge. Central banks can see settlement, but not necessarily the upstream belief formation that triggered the flow.

Second, intervention latency becomes visible. Rules are clear, but adaptation is slow. By the time governance reacts, behaviour has already propagated.

Third, incentive misalignment surfaces. Commercial banks are asked to absorb operational and marketing costs, as in the case of China's interest-bearing e-CNY via banks, without controlling the intelligence layer that drives usage.

This is not a failure of technology.
It is a mismatch of incentives.

## Permissioned versus permissionless

The lesson of cross-border CBDC pilots is that central banks are trying to solve yesterday's problem. They are optimising for who gets to stop the system, not for who gets to move it fastest. In an AI-mediated world, that distinction becomes decisive.

Payments infrastructure that cannot be observed in real time, classified behaviourally, and interrupted when confidence breaks is not safe, no matter how fast it settles.

This is what makes SWIFT's 2025 decision so revealing.

When SWIFT announced that its move into tokenised payment processing would be built on a permissionless[48], Ethereum-based platform, it was not endorsing decentralisation ideology. It was acknowledging an execution reality.

SWIFT understands something the CBDC pilots are still carefully avoiding: the fact that future payment flows will not be confined to pre-negotiated corridors. They will be routed dynamically by machines across multiple rails, assets, and jurisdictions, based on price, confidence, and execution certainty.

Choosing a controlled settlement substrate based on a permissionless platform does not mean abandoning control. It means accepting that control must move up the stack — away from who is allowed to participate, and toward how behaviour is observed, classified, and interrupted in real time.

In effect, SWIFT is conceding that messaging logic alone is no longer sufficient. In an AI-mediated world, payments infrastructure must behave like an executable fabric, not a negotiated pathway.

That choice puts SWIFT closer to how AI systems actually operate than most sovereign CBDC designs — not because it is more radical, but because it is more pragmatic.

And that is why the AI Bank must treat payments not as plumbing, but as governance made executable.

## Payments in an Agent-Mediated World

The next payments revolution will not be announced as a new wallet.

It will arrive as a change in who initiates transactions.

In the digital era, payments were still user-driven. The customer clicked. The merchant requested. The bank authorised. The rails moved money. The interface changed, but the choreography remained recognisable.

In the agentic era, the choreography changes. The user delegates intent. The agent executes the journey. Payments become a callable function inside a broader workflow: "buy", "renew", "refund", "rebalance", "insure", "book", "ship".

That is why protocols are becoming the real battlefield.

Google's launch of the Universal Commerce Protocol (UCP) is a clear signal of where the market is heading: an attempt to standardise how agents and merchants negotiate discovery, checkout, payments, and post-purchase support[49]. Whether UCP becomes dominant is not the immediate point. The point is that commerce is being redesigned so agents can complete transactions without humans visiting a website or navigating a checkout flow.

This shifts the role of payments players.

Checkout was where payment brands captured attention and where merchants optimised conversion. If the agent becomes the checkout, attention moves upstream to identity, permissioning, and risk. The transaction becomes less visible. The trust layer becomes more important.

It also changes fraud.

Most fraud systems were built around human behaviour: device fingerprints, typing patterns, browsing paths, location anomalies. Agents will not behave like humans. They will behave like code. Transaction velocity, tool-call patterns, and capability usage anomalies become the new signals. Consent becomes a machine-readable artefact rather than a remembered click.

For banks, this is the uncomfortable reality: the bank may still provide the account, the authorisation, and the recourse, but it will increasingly be asked to execute within flows it did not design. The customer experience will be mediated by someone else's agent and someone else's interface.

That is why "agent trust" becomes a core payments competency. Know Your Customer will not be enough. The system will need to know the agent acting on the customer's behalf, prove authorisation, and log the chain of intent and execution.

In the agentic payments world, the bank is not competing to own the wallet. It is competing to be the most trusted execution engine inside an invisible workflow.

## The legacy card players

It is worth paying close attention to how senior executives from the legacy payments platforms now choose their words, because their institutional positions shape what they can afford to say.

When Jack Forestell, Chief Product Officer at Visa, talks about the future of payments, he is speaking as the executive responsible for a global network built decades ago around batch authorisation, delayed settlement, and human-mediated dispute resolution[50]. His emphasis on AI-driven authorisation, network-level risk scoring, and real-time decisioning reflects a defensive structural bias: if intelligence migrates away from the network, Visa risks being reduced to a commoditised clearing utility, which technically is what its rails are today.

A similar logic underpins how Michael Miebach, Chief Executive Officer of Mastercard, frames Mastercard's evolution. Miebach rose through Mastercard's data and product businesses[51]. His focus on identity, fraud, cybersecurity, and AI-driven insights reflects an institutional reality: card rails alone are no longer sufficient. Both Mastercard and Visa will have a gigantic challenge of inserting themselves into the decision layer of payments if they want to remain indispensable.

Both implicitly acknowledge that cards were never designed for an agentic world.

Legacy card rails strain most visibly in Africa and parts of Asia, where mobile-first behaviour dominates and liquidity is fragile.

Batch reconciliation, delayed settlement, and FX friction are poorly suited to environments where payments are behavioural, not episodic. This is why new cross-border payment platforms continue to emerge across these regions, combining mobile money, real-time settlement, and local currency corridors that challenge the legacy card players. The innovations underway at MPesa will be instructive as to whether some of the AI breakthroughs in payments will comes from Africa rather than the West.

## PayPal and Stripe: Two Diverging AI Futures

PayPal and Stripe illustrate two very different responses to the same pressure.

PayPal, now led by Alex Chriss, sits in an awkward middle ground. It is neither a bank nor pure infrastructure. Its historical strength was consumer trust layered on top of existing rails. PayPal's AI strategy focuses heavily on fraud detection, identity assurance, and personalization[52]. These are defensive moves, aimed at preserving relevance as checkout itself becomes invisible.

PayPal uses AI to remain present at the moment of transaction, even as that moment dissolves.

Stripe occupies a fundamentally different position.

Stripe, led by Patrick Collison, was built as a developer-first execution layer from the start. Payments were treated as an API problem, not a consumer experience[53]. Stripe's use of AI is deeply embedded in fraud prevention, dispute management, pricing optimisation, and increasingly autonomous financial operations for platforms and marketplaces.

Stripe's bias is infrastructural. Its future customer is not a human clicking "pay", but an agent, a platform, or a piece of software acting continuously.

PayPal uses AI to defend the edge.
Stripe uses AI to dissolve payments into infrastructure.

Only one of these trajectories aligns cleanly with an agentic future.

## Can India's UPI scale intelligence?

India's Unified Payments Interface (UPI) is rightly celebrated as one of the world's most successful real-time retail payment systems. Combined with Aadhaar, it created a uniquely powerful substrate: identity, authentication, and payment at population scale[54].

The question now is not whether UPI works. It is what UPI becomes when AI sits on top of it.

With AI, payments stop being initiated by humans tapping screens. They are initiated by agents acting on context: cash flow, eligibility, behavioural patterns, and risk signals. Credit, subsidies, pricing, and limits can all be adjusted dynamically.

The opportunity for inclusion is enormous.
So is the risk of automated exclusion and manufactured eligibility.

From the Reserve Bank of India's perspective, the bias has always been stability-first[55]. That bias will be tested. UPI with AI is not just faster payments. It is national-scale delegated judgement, and it requires observability and intervention capabilities that go far beyond what exists today.

## China: The state versus agentic AI tension

China offers a lesson that is often misunderstood outside the country.

WeChat Pay and Alipay were not merely successful payment tools. They became full-fledged superapps in the *platform era* because they solved a very specific problem: they unified identity, messaging, commerce, payments, credit, and daily services inside a single, closed interface[56]. In doing so, they captured attention, context, and behaviour at population scale. They did not just process transactions; they mediated everyday life.

This is why they worked.

In a world where humans were still the primary initiators of action, owning the interface meant owning intent. The superapp was powerful because it was where users spent time, where decisions were framed, and where execution naturally followed. In that sense, WeChat Pay and Alipay perfected the platform model. They were not banks, but they effectively governed financial behaviour more directly than banks ever could.

From a pure AI perspective, these systems already look proto-agentic. They infer intent from behaviour, price risk dynamically, embed credit at the moment of action, and coordinate multiple services without explicit user instruction. In many respects, they remain far ahead of most banks globally.

Ironically, this success is precisely why the Chinese state intervened.

The introduction of the e-CNY, now the world's largest retail central bank digital currency experiment[57], was never just about digitising cash. It was an attempt to reclaim visibility and control over a payments and behavioural ecosystem that had become too intelligent, too fast, and too centralised outside direct state reach. The concern was not innovation; it was sovereignty over execution.

What is often missed is that the state was responding to a *platform-era* concentration problem. WeChat and Alipay had become superapps because they controlled the interface. The state's instinctive response was therefore to compete at the same layer: issue a sovereign payment instrument, mandate distribution through banks, and reassert hierarchical control.

But the world has already moved on.

The most recent decision to make the e-CNY interest-bearing via commercial banks exposes the tension clearly. Banks were effectively asked to shoulder the marketing, onboarding, and distribution costs of a state-sponsored tokenised payment system in order to advance what remains a sovereign control objective. Adoption has been limited, not because the technology fails, but because the governance logic is misaligned with how intelligence now operates.

This is not a failure of digital currency design. It is a mismatch of eras.

In the AI world, the superapp is no longer defined by a single destination interface. Intelligence no longer requires users to live inside one application. Instead, it operates above applications, orchestrating across services, protocols, and data sources. The new "superapp" is not a container; it is an agentic layer.

In this paradigm, power shifts away from owning the interface and toward owning orchestration: who defines context, who controls execution rules, who can route decisions across systems, and who retains stop-power when behaviour accelerates. Superapps in the AI era are not closed ecosystems. They are coordination engines.

This is where the Chinese state faces a structural challenge.

Central banks are built for hierarchical control, explicit permissions, and human-paced governance. AI systems, by contrast, favour programmable execution, continuous negotiation, and decentralised coordination. The e-CNY reflects the former logic; agentic commerce reflects the latter. The tension is therefore not ideological. It is architectural.

WeChat Pay and Alipay succeeded because they mastered the superapp model of the platform era[58]. The state's response assumes that the same model can simply be reasserted with sovereign authority. But in an agentic world, the winning superapps will not be places users go. They will be systems that act on users' behalf, across platforms, invisibly, and continuously.

That is why the struggle over payments in China is no longer just about public versus private control. It is about whether governance can adapt from managing interfaces to managing behaviour. AI wants execution to be programmable and portable. Central banks want control to remain centralised and explicit.

That tension will not resolve cleanly. And China is simply encountering it earlier, and at far greater scale, than anyone else.

## M-Pesa: From Mobile Money to AI Infrastructure

M-Pesa began as a simple mobile money system. It became a national and now international infrastructure[59].

As AI enters the picture, M-Pesa evolves again.

In my conversations with the head of IT of M-Pesa, I get the sense that with AI-driven risk assessment and contextual credit, M-Pesa is becoming a behavioural operating system[60]. Loans, limits, and pricing adjust dynamically. Payments reflect confidence signals rather than static rules.

The upside is inclusion at scale.
The downside is belief-driven cascades.

When M-Pesa becomes AI-driven, Kenya's payments system will become a live experiment in national-scale delegated judgement.

Put all of this together and the direction becomes clear.

Payments are becoming autonomous, contextual, agent-driven, programmable, and politically sensitive.

In the AI Bank, payments are not plumbing.
They are governance made executable.

Institutions that treat payments as rails will lose control.
Institutions that treat payments as prudential control surfaces will shape the system.

That is why payments are where control is tested first, and why everything that follows in this book depends on how that test is answered.

# CHAPTER SIX

# AI as an Operating System

*"People in college use ChatGPT as an operating system."*
*– Sam Altman*[61]

---

Many banks are beginning their AI journey in the safest possible place: horizontal tools. Productivity copilots. Document summarisation. Conversational interfaces.

They feel safe because they sit far away from the real pinch of AI on the institution.

They also teach the institution almost nothing.

Horizontal tools create visible activity without forcing clarity about decision rights, escalation paths, or accountability. They delay the moment when the bank must confront what it is actually willing to let machines decide.

Real AI capability is built vertically, around decision surfaces that matter: payment routing, liquidity allocation, fraud intervention, credit limit adjustment, exception handling. These are the points where judgement becomes irreversible.

Those surfaces force the institution to wire control before scale.

Banks that treat AI as a programme eventually ask the wrong question: how many use cases have we deployed?

AI banks ask a different question: how many material decisions are now machine-supported, and how are they governed?

This is why AI is not a software upgrade to an existing architecture. It reshapes how the institution senses, decides, acts, and intervenes. Once execution is automated, especially through payments, there is no safe sandbox.

The system is live.

If the AI stack defines what must exist, architecture determines who controls it. Control over data, inference, decision boundaries, and execution cannot be outsourced without outsourcing judgement itself. Once execution moves at machine speed, rented intelligence becomes institutional risk.

## The Real AI Stack of a Bank

Let us be clear about one thing. AI in banking does not begin with chatbots.

Chatbots are theatre. They sit at the surface. They reassure boards. They impress customers. They leave power exactly where it has always been.

The real question is simpler, and far more uncomfortable: where does intelligence sit when money moves?

Payments will no longer be messaging systems. They will become execution environments. When value moves at machine speed, intelligence is no longer advisory. It is operational.

That reality forces a redesign of the bank's internal stack.

The AI Stack is not a technology stack. Banks often describe their AI efforts in technical layers: data, models, platforms, tools. That framing misses the point.

The real AI stack of a bank is functional, not technical. It describes how signals become decisions, how decisions become action, and how action is supervised.

An AI bank has four irreducible layers: Data, Inference, Control, and Execution.

This is not an abstract model. It is the minimum structure required to prevent intelligence from outrunning accountability. It is, in effect, the new core banking system.

### 1. Data: Seeing the Present, Not the Past

Data in an AI bank is not a warehouse of historical truth. It is a live representation of the institution's operating environment.

Signals arrive continuously: customer behaviour, liquidity flows, network conditions, counterparty activity, market movements. The value of data decays rapidly. What matters is not completeness, but timeliness and relevance.

This is why AI banks care less about data lakes and more about data readiness: lineage, provenance, latency, and integrity. If the system cannot trust its inputs in real time, no downstream control is possible.

### 2. Inference: Forming Belief at Machine Speed

Inference is where the bank forms beliefs: about intent, risk, opportunity, and next action.

These beliefs are probabilistic, not deterministic. They update continuously as new signals arrive. They are shaped by incentives, training data, and feedback loops.

This is the layer where most banks currently concentrate their AI investment. It is also the layer where most failures begin.

Inference is seductive because it feels powerful. But inference without constraint does not create advantage. It creates fragility.

### 3. Context Is the Differentiator

A revealing signal came not from a bank, but from consumer technology.

In 2025, Apple made a decision that would have been unthinkable a decade earlier. Rather than insist on building its own frontier language models end-to-end, Apple chose to integrate external intelligence from Google, using Gemini to power the next generation of Siri.

For Apple, this was not a failure of ambition.
It was a statement of architecture.

Apple is the most vertically integrated consumer technology company in the world. It designs its own silicon, controls its operating systems, governs its app ecosystem, and obsessively protects user data. It has historically treated external dependence as a strategic weakness.

And yet, when it came to large language models, Apple chose not to compete on model supremacy.

Because Apple understood something many institutions still resist: the model is not the differentiator. The context is.

Apple already owns one of the richest context layers ever assembled: messages, calendars, photos, contacts, application behaviour, device signals, and location history, all bound together by identity, hardware control, and user consent. That context is real-time, deeply personal, and extraordinarily difficult to replicate.

What Apple elected to outsource was not judgement.
It outsourced inference.

This distinction matters.

Inference can be rented, upgraded, swapped, and benchmarked. Large language models increasingly behave like utilities: expensive to train, broadly accessible, and converging in capability. Their marginal advantage erodes quickly.

Context does not.

Context is accumulated slowly. It is governed by trust, permissions, integration discipline, and continuity over time. It is where intent becomes legible and where execution becomes meaningful. Without context, even the most capable model is reduced to a clever generalist with no authority to act.

Apple's decision makes explicit what many AI teams discover only after repeated failure. Agents do not break because models are weak. They break because context is fragmented. Data is siloed. Permissions are unclear. Execution surfaces are disconnected.

A brilliant model operating without context is useless.
A modest model operating inside rich context is powerful.

This is the inversion most organisations miss.

Apple is not betting on superior intelligence.
It is betting on superior infrastructure.

And that choice exposes a deeper truth for banks.

### 4. Control: The Decision Boundary

Control is a passive activity in digital banking. It is active in an AI bank.

It is where the institution decides what the system is allowed to do, under what conditions, and with what escalation paths.

Control translates policy into executable constraints: limits, thresholds, confidence requirements, kill switches, fallback modes, and human override authority.

This layer does not optimise outcomes.

It preserves legitimacy.

When inference slips past control, speed outruns accountability.
When control suffocates inference, paralysis is mistaken for safety.

This boundary — not the ledger or the app — is now the true core of banking.

## Models Do Not Create Power

For decades, banks believed that owning the core system meant owning the customer. Then platforms proved that distribution could be lost while balance sheets remained.

AI introduces a harsher inversion.

A bank can own capital, licences, and models, yet still lose control over when and how its balance sheet is activated.

In an AI bank, the equivalent of Apple's context layer is not the model. It is the live financial reality of the customer: transaction history, cash-flow cadence, obligations, behavioural signals, permissions, and the right to act at the moment intent crystallises.

That context increasingly sits outside the institution, fragmented across wallets, platforms, devices, and agents the bank does not control.

This is why banks that focus their AI strategy on "owning the model" are repeating the mistake of the digital era. They defend an internal asset while external systems define execution.

The model may recommend.
The bank may approve.
But the decision has already happened elsewhere.

A bank that rents inference but owns execution surfaces can remain central.
A bank that owns inference but rents context becomes a utility.

This is the real build-versus-buy question banks should be asking. Not whether to train models internally, but whether they are prepared to engineer, govern, and defend the context layer that determines when money moves.

In finance, unlike consumer technology, the cost of losing that layer is not relevance. It is systemic risk.

Inference therefore has to be tested, rehearsed, and retuned constantly — at board level, management level, and operational level. It becomes the religion of the bank.

## Execution: Where Payments Change Everything

Banks have spent a decade talking about data. The next decade will be defined by execution.

In the digital era, a bank could afford to treat execution as plumbing. Payments were processed, disputes were handled, reconciliations were performed, and the institution's real differentiation was placed elsewhere: distribution, branding, product bundles, relationship management.

AI compresses those separations.

The moment an agent can connect analysis to action, execution becomes the product. Routing decisions, collateral shifts, liquidity rebalancing, and payment initiation stop being operational details and become competitive capabilities.

This is why the payments layer is not simply being modernised. It is being pulled upward into orchestration.

When an AI system can decide and initiate within the same workflow, the bank's execution environment becomes its most valuable asset: the place where intent is converted into legally final movement of value. That environment must be designed to accept agentic initiation without losing control. It must enforce policy at the moment of action, not after the incident.

This is also why standards are so consequential. When orchestration layers can call tools across providers using common protocols, they can treat payment execution as a modular capability. Banks that cannot expose execution safely, with strong controls and auditable trails, will not be selected by agents. They will not be in the workflow.

The AI Bank is not the one with the smartest assistant. It is the one with the safest execution boundary.

## The Data Outside the Bank

A bank's balance sheet is inside the institution.

But the bank's reality increasingly sits outside it.

The data that shapes credit decisions, fraud detection, suitability, and customer intent is no longer generated mainly by banking interactions. It is generated by networks: commerce platforms, communications platforms, device ecosystems, employer systems, and now the orchestration layers that mediate work.

This is where the interface shift becomes existential.

Liquidity no longer resides primarily on balance sheets. It follows information.

It sits in wallets, platforms, protocols, corporate treasuries, tokenised pools, and increasingly in machine-to-machine environments. This is not a temporary displacement. It is a permanent reconfiguration.

Liquidity follows information.

As behavioural signals, intent, and execution cues migrate outward, liquidity follows them. AI accelerates this process by discovering, aggregating, and mobilising dormant liquidity faster than traditional intermediation can.

Banks that treat external liquidity as a threat defend shrinking perimeters.
Banks that treat it as a resource to be orchestrated retain relevance.

When tasks are performed inside an AI interface that can render and invoke other applications, the orchestration layer sees the sequence of intent. It sees the "why" behind actions, not just the transactions that result. It becomes the place where context is assembled, refreshed, and acted upon.

For banks, the danger is not that they lack data. It is that they lack the right to interpret and use the data that defines the customer's life. And in regulated environments, the ability to see data is inseparable from the duty to govern it: consent, retention, auditability, suitability, and dispute resolution.

This is why context architecture is not a technical add-on. It is strategic.

If a bank's AI depends on context that is assembled outside its control, the bank becomes downstream of someone else's worldview. It will be asked to execute decisions derived from context it did not curate, cannot fully audit, and may not be permitted to store.

The AI Bank must therefore be able to do two things at once:
it must connect to outside context so it can remain relevant, and it must enforce an internal decision boundary so it can remain accountable.

That is the difference between being interoperable and being absorbed.

## Why Ring-Fencing Fails in an AI World

Traditional regulatory and organisational responses assume separability: ring-fence the balance sheet, isolate activities, segment risk.

That approach became fashionable after the global financial crisis not because of some intellectual epiphany, but simply because the data systems finally allowed it.

AI destroys separability.

When intelligence is trained on enterprise-wide data and acts across workflows, decisions made in one part of the institution inevitably affect outcomes elsewhere. Information does not respect legal entities, booking locations, or reporting lines.

Ring-fencing may remain politically expedient, but it is no longer operationally safe.

The only viable control mechanism is decision-boundary enforcement: explicit constraints on what models can infer, recommend, and execute, regardless of where data originates.

Control moves from structure to behaviour and this will redefine finance for the foreseeable future.

## Trust Becomes Machine-Readable

Trust has always been the central currency of banking, but for most of its history it was expressed socially rather than technically. Trust lived in institutions, in brands, in regulatory charters, and in the assumption that humans were making judgments in good faith, subject to oversight.

Digital systems began to formalise trust, but only partially. Authentication verified identity. Encryption protected transmission. Logs recorded actions after the fact. Yet much of the system still relied on implicit assumptions: that a user was who they claimed to be, that a click represented intent, that a human sat behind the keyboard.

Agentic systems break those assumptions.

When AI agents initiate actions, trust can no longer be inferred from behaviour. It must be proven, continuously, and in machine-readable form. The system must know not only *who* is acting, but *what* is acting, *on whose behalf*, *with what authority*, and *under which constraints*.

This is the point at which trust stops being a narrative and becomes an artifact.

In an agent-mediated world, trust is expressed through credentials, permissions, policies, and attestations. It is enforced through protocols, not promises. Consent is no longer a remembered click; it is a cryptographically verifiable mandate. Authority is not assumed; it is scoped, time-bound, revocable, and logged.

This matters because the speed and scale of AI decision-making collapses traditional control mechanisms. When thousands of micro-decisions are made per second, there is no room for after-the-fact explanations. The system must be defensible at the moment of action.

Machine-readable trust enables that.

It allows institutions to define what an agent may do, not just what it may see. It allows regulators to audit how decisions were produced, not merely what outcomes occurred. And it allows banks to expose execution capabilities to agents without surrendering control.

Crucially, this is not about removing humans from accountability. It is about making accountability legible when humans are no longer present at every step.

In the AI Bank, trust is not something you assert.
It is something the system can prove.

# CHAPTER SEVEN

# New Products for a New Age

*"People don't know what they want until you show it to them."*
*– Steve Jobs*[62]

---

I often say in my speeches and definitely in my first book, that in any industry, if the products do not change, nothing changed.

Digital banking did not fall short because the technology was inadequate.

It failed because the product never changed.

Banks digitised distribution, redesigned interfaces, and automated workflows, but left the underlying product logic intact. Accounts, loans, cards, and investment wrappers were delivered faster and cheaper, but they were still the same products.

This is the part banks consistently misunderstood in the digital era.

They believed digitisation meant putting existing products onto better screens. They redesigned channels but never learned how to extract value from information itself. Fintechs made the same mistake. They assumed that new distribution would create new products. It did not. It created cheaper, faster versions of old ones.

Information was treated as exhaust: something to support a transaction, not something to be priced, packaged, or sold in its own right.

AI exposes this failure brutally.

In an AI Bank, products are no longer static instruments. They are conversations, commitments, and executable states. More precisely, they are ways of organising, pricing, and acting on information.

AI changes this because it turns information from exhaust into the primary economic input.

## Ghosts from A Digital Past

The AI era does not arrive on a blank slate. It inherits a landscape shaped by fintechs that solved real problems in the digital era.

Peer-to-peer lending platforms were the first visible crack in the product catalogue. Platforms such as Zopa[63] and LendingClub[64] succeeded not because they reinvented credit, but because they reframed finance as a matching problem rather than a product sale.

Borrowers did not want a "loan product." They wanted funding for a purpose. Lenders did not want a savings account. They wanted exposure with transparency.

P2P collapsed those intents into a single flow.

But its limitation was structural. When risk rose, liquidity vanished. When defaults increased, platforms discovered that someone still had to absorb loss. Balance sheets did not disappear. They were merely displaced.

Peer-to-peer proved that finance could be disaggregated from banks — but not from risk, unless the product was something else. Like information.

Buy Now, Pay Later went further.

Providers like Klarna[65], Afterpay, and Affirm[66] did not market themselves as lenders. They embedded credit directly into the act of purchase. Their underwriting logic remained thin, their settlement depended on legacy rails, and their risk intelligence was largely derivative of transactional data.

Credit appeared at the moment of commitment.

The customer did not apply.
They did not compare APRs.
They did not even think of it as borrowing.

Credit appeared at the moment of commitment.

This was a decisive break from the banking product catalogue.

BNPL demonstrated that finance is most powerful when it is situational, not when it is sold. It also demonstrated the limits of that approach. As volumes grew, regulators intervened. Losses accumulated. Funding costs rose. Providers were forced either to partner with banks or to behave like them.

Again, the pattern repeated.

Finance could dissolve into life — but risk always re-consolidated somewhere else, and this is a point worth carrying into an AI Bank.

Many alternative credit models already behaved like early agents.

They:

- inferred intent from behaviour
- priced risk in real time
- executed decisions instantly
- reversed or escalated when signals changed

What they lacked was governance at scale, and to bring us back to my point that this was always a balance sheet goal.

They operated as point solutions rather than institutional systems. When stress arrived, they discovered that execution without restraint is fragility, not innovation.

This is why BNPL, P2P, and alternative credit ultimately gravitated back toward banks — not because banks were faster, but because banks were built to absorb loss and provide recourse.

That gravitational pull never disappeared. The competitive frontier is alignment, Not engagement. In a life-infrastructure model, banks no longer compete for attention. They compete for alignment.

Customer agents remember:

- which institutions executed reliably
- which priced fairly under stress
- which reversed errors cleanly
- which honoured constraints rather than gaming them

This is not brand loyalty.
It is behavioural preference.

The bank is chosen because it behaves predictably when execution is unavoidable. This was a decisive break from the banking product catalogue. BNPL demonstrated that finance is most powerful when it is situational, not when it is sold.

But in an AI world, that imbalance is fatal.

BNPL will not disappear. It will dissolve into embedded credit intelligence inside larger agentic systems.

Most successful fintechs of the digital era were built around human choice: better UX, clearer pricing, faster onboarding.

AI removes humans from the critical path.

When agents decide, fintechs no longer compete on experience. They compete on machine-readable rules, execution certainty, and informational advantage.

In that world, some fintechs become capabilities inside larger agentic system. Some become regulated execution utilities. A few evolve into full AI-native financial institutions

The determining factor is not brand, valuation, or customer count.

It is whether the institution understands that information itself is the product — and whether it can operate at the execution layer where decisions become irreversible.

Neobanks like Revolut won the interface war of the digital era. But in an AI world, the interface stops being the battlefield.

As payments, FX, and liquidity routing become machine-mediated, customer agents care less about super-apps and more about execution certainty, observability, and reversibility.

Revolut's challenge is not scaling users. It is deciding where intelligence and control sit.

If intelligence remains concentrated in the app layer while execution and decision boundaries live elsewhere, the institution risks becoming the UI of the AI Bank — not the Bank.

Cross-border specialists like Wise solved opaque FX pricing by re-engineering transparency while relying on existing banking rails. In an AI world, FX stops being a product and becomes a continuous optimisation function, executed automatically by agents.

Wise can evolve into an execution primitive embedded in agentic routing, or remain a visible product competing for human attention. The former requires deep integration into the execution layer. The latter risks marginalisation.

## Digital Assets Are Not Products Either

Banks now speak of "digital assets" as if they are a new product category. They are not.

Digital assets are containers. What matters is what they allow information to do: move, recombine, signal, and settle without friction.

Treating tokens as products repeats the same mistake banks made with APIs and mobile apps.

In an AI Bank, tokens are not sold.
They are used — to carry identity, permissions, state, and value across environments.

The product is not the token.
The product is the information flow it enables.

## "The Conversation is the Product"

It is a theme that I have been repeating like a mantra all along. Finally, generative AI and agents now make this a reality.

In an AI Bank, the conversation is not marketing.
It is not customer service.
It is not sentiment analysis.

The conversation is the product.

Fintech barons always thought they understood this, but what they meant was better engagement, better targeting, better UX. That framing was incomplete.

What has changed is not the existence of conversation.
It is what can now be done with it.

Peer-to-peer platforms, BNPL providers, and early alternative credit models all sat close to human intent. Borrowers explained why they needed funds. Lenders expressed preferences. Communities discussed opportunities and risks. The products sat right there in the conversations, but those conversations were ignored by the system.

They were not structured.
They were not interpreted.
They were not executable.

Early P2P platforms matched capital. They did not learn from the ample conversations on their platforms. That is why products still had to be predefined, priced in advance, and sold as objects rather than assembled as responses.

Once conversation becomes structured, learnable, and executable, the product catalogue collapses.

There is no need to design dozens of static offerings when products can be assembled instantly, pricing can reflect context, execution can be reversed, and outcomes can be supervised.

The product is no longer the loan, the BNPL plan, or the account. The product is the bank's ability to listen, interpret, and act correctly. Products are no longer invented in committees.

They are discovered in conversation and assembled when intent becomes real.

Once finance becomes life infrastructure, products lose their meaning.

What remains are capabilities:

- liquidity when commitment arises
- credit when timing matters
- protection when exposure appears
- reversibility when systems are wrong

These capabilities are assembled dynamically, often across institutions, and executed by agents under constraint.

The customer does not choose products.
Their agent negotiates execution.

## Reddit and the Pre-Product Signal

The early 2020s provided an unmistakable signal. This is also why community conversation suddenly matters in a way it never did before.

The explosion of financial discourse on Reddit — most visibly during the GameStop episode — demonstrated that collective conversation itself could move markets, mobilise capital, and reshape risk perception in real time.

Platforms such as Reddit, Discord, Slack and even Telegram have long been full of latent financial demand: discussions about housing stress, medical expenses, income volatility, education costs, side businesses, and risk management. Historically, these conversations produced sentiment, not solutions.

Banks dismissed this as noise, speculation, or distortion. They missed the deeper lesson.

Those conversations were not commentary. They were pre-product signals: expressions of intent, belief, frustration, aspiration, and coordination.

Their potent power was illustrated in the GameStop short-squeeze, when folks in a Reddit sub-community called WallStreetBets, essentially took on the big hedge funds[67].

At the time, no institution could reliably transform that conversation into governed execution without crossing ethical or regulatory lines.

AI changes that boundary.

When conversation can be parsed, clustered, and interpreted responsibly, it becomes diagnostic rather than promotional. It reveals emerging needs early enough for finance to respond — not reactively, but proactively, under constraint.

This is where life infrastructure replaces product design. The system does not wait for a customer to ask for credit. It recognises the conditions under which credit may soon be required, and prepares options accordingly.

The conversation does not become the product because it persuades.
It becomes the product because it is diagnostic.

## Products as life management

A quiet but important signal arrived when OpenAI acquired the team behind ROl, an application that combined financial aggregation with a command-centre view of assets, cash, and trading activity.[68]

This was not a move to build a bank.

It was a move to absorb finance into life management.

ROl did not present a catalogue of financial products. It presented a situational view of money: what resources were available, what risks were present, what commitments were upcoming, and what actions could be taken now.

That distinction matters.

When OpenAI frames finance as part of "life management," it is signalling a structural shift. Finance stops being a destination[69]. It becomes infrastructure, invoked automatically when intent appears elsewhere.

The user does not log into a bank. They log into their own lives.

The AI system decides when finance must surface.

It treated money as something to be managed continuously, in context, alongside other life decisions. When OpenAI framed finance as part of "life management," it was signalling that banking functions are becoming background capabilities, invoked automatically when intent appears elsewhere.

This is the same trajectory P2P and BNPL hinted at — now executed with far greater intelligence.

The user does not log into a bank.
They log into everyday life.

Finance surfaces only when required.

That trajectory becomes unmistakable with agentic commerce which is already a reality.

Also inside ChatGPT, in agentic commerce, a user in the US can already discover a product, commit to purchase, and complete payment entirely inside a conversation, supported by Shopify and merchants including Etsy.

There is no product selection phase.
There is no checkout page.
There is only intent, followed by execution.

BNPL embedded credit into checkout.
Agentic commerce embeds checkout into intent.

The direction is clear.

Deposits cease to be storage. They become liquidity interfaces.

Credit becomes a capsule: a live bundle of behaviour, collateral, context, and execution rules.
Investing becomes continuous risk choreography.
Payments become decisions realised — execution certainty under constraint.
Insurance becomes a real-time negotiation of risk boundaries.

The product is no longer the wrapper. It is the behaviour of the institution. These capabilities are assembled dynamically and executed by agents under constraint.

The customer does not choose products.
Their agent negotiates execution.

## Products Ruled by Permissions

There is another side to the mantra that the conversation is the product. Banks now have to overcome customer's permission.

When customers can define what information flows into an agent, the "product" is no longer an account, a loan, or a dashboard. It is permission: what the agent is allowed to see, how often it updates, and under what conditions it may act.

This is why earlier fintech models stalled. They redesigned interfaces, but they never surrendered control over context.

MCP-style access breaks that monopoly. Model Context Protocols explain why products dissolve so quickly in an AI world.

In a life-infrastructure model, banks do not ship products.
They expose controlled, legible execution surfaces that agents can plug into.

That is the new product boundary that is counter to the instinct of a banker.

## The Product Strategy of the AI Bank

Traditional banking is reactive.

A customer applies. A product is approved. Execution follows.

In an AI Bank, finance becomes proactively assembled.

When conversations indicate rising stress, upcoming commitments, or latent exposure, agents can prepare responses before a formal request is made — subject to consent, constraints, and stop-power.

Liquidity is staged. Risk is pre-hedged. Options are surfaced early.

This is not manipulation. It is anticipatory alignment.

The ethical boundary is not proactivity.

It is whether the system acts for the customer or at the customer.

In an AI world, banks are surrounded by information: behavioural signals, intent, context, network position, transaction patterns, and predictive insight.

The limiting factor is no longer data collection.
It is product imagination.

AI-native products share four characteristics:

- They monetise information directly, not just the financial instrument it supports
- They evolve continuously rather than being originated and held
- They are negotiated by agents, not selected from menus
- They generate value even when no transaction occurs

This is a radical departure from digital banking logic.

In an AI Bank, the interface is intent.

Products emerge from dialogue between agents. Pricing, suitability, risk, and duration are negotiated continuously. There is no fixed moment of sale.

This is why product design can no longer sit downstream of technology or marketing. It must sit at the intersection of information, execution, and governance.

Banks that continue to design products as static offerings will be invisible to machine-mediated customers. Banks that learn to design products around information — how it is generated, trusted, acted upon, and priced — will define the next era of finance. Once products become executable, leadership can no longer hide behind structure.

When machines decide, the institution must answer a question it can no longer defer: Who is accountable?

The AI Bank does not design products. It designs:

- listening
- interpretation
- constraint
- execution
- reversal

It does not ask, *"What should we sell?"*
It asks, *"What is life asking for right now?"*

That is the end of the product catalogue, and the beginning of finance as life infrastructure.

The AI Bank also designs:

- constraints
- guarantees
- execution reliability
- reversibility

It does not ask, *"What should we sell?"*
It asks, *"Under what conditions do we act?"*

That is the end of the product catalogue.

And the beginning of finance as life infrastructure.

# CHAPTER EIGHT

# Agents from Apps to Actors

*"What would you do if you were beautiful?"*
*– Sally Bowles in the musical Cabaret*[70]

---

In digital banking, software supported decisions. In the AI Bank, it is the agents that observe signals, form beliefs, infer intent, operate within constraints, and increasingly execute actions. They represent customers, relationship managers, treasury desks, risk functions, and sometimes the institution itself.

In the earlier chapter, I described the AI stack as moving from data to inference, from inference to control, and from control to execution.

Agents are where those layers collapse into behaviour. Products defined digital banking. Agents define AI banking. An app is passive. An agent acts.

This distinction is not cosmetic. It marks the moment intelligence stops advising humans and starts operating the institution.

They do not sit neatly inside reporting lines or product silos. They operate across the AI stack. That is why agents are not a feature. They are an organisational unit.

An agent ingests live data. It forms inferences about intent, risk, or opportunity. It operates within control boundaries defined by policy. And it executes actions, often through payments.

This is not automation. It is delegated judgement.

Once agents exist, authority no longer flows only through hierarchy. It flows through constraints. The institution no longer asks, *"Who approved this?"* It must answer, *"Under what conditions was this allowed to happen?"*

That is the shift most banks are not yet prepared for.

## From Tools to Actors

Most banks still deploy AI as tools.

Chat interfaces.
Copilots.
Recommendation engines.

These systems assist humans. They speed up work. They improve productivity. They rarely change how the bank behaves under stress. Agents do.

Agents initiate workflows, sequence actions, recover from errors, escalate when confidence drops, and interact with other agents inside and outside the institution.

This is why agentic AI matters more than bigger models.

The AI pioneer, Andrew Ng has repeatedly emphasised that the real shift in AI is from generation to execution[71]. Large language models generate text. Agents generate outcomes.

In banking, this distinction is already visible.

Onboarding is no longer a conversation. It is a sequence.
Fraud response is no longer a rule. It is a chain of actions.
Liquidity management is no longer a report. It is a continuous intervention loop.

Agents turn these sequences into living systems. What changed quietly in late 2025 was not that agents became more capable. It was that they became boring.

A system released by Anthropic illustrated this shift with unsettling clarity[72]. The product was not presented as a breakthrough in reasoning or a new interface for prompting. It did something far more consequential.

An agent was given access to a working environment.
It was given a goal.
It was allowed to operate.

The agent planned its own sequence of actions. It read files, reorganised information, generated documents, corrected its own errors, asked clarifying questions when confidence dropped, and continued until the task was complete. There was no step-by-step prompting. No copy-pasting between applications. No human babysitting disguised as oversight.

This was not assistance.
It was delegation.

What made this moment decisive was not sophistication, but persistence. The agent did not reset after each response. It carried state across time. It remembered what it had already done, noticed when something failed, repaired the workflow, and resumed execution. This is the point at which software stops behaving like a tool and starts behaving like a worker.

Crucially, the system did not rely on trust by declaration. It ran inside a constrained execution environment. Human interruption was available by default. Action could be paused, inspected, or stopped. Governance was not layered on top of autonomy; it was embedded into the act of execution itself.

This is the practical meaning of agentic AI.

An agent that can observe context, form a plan, execute across multiple systems, recover from error, and remain interruptible is no longer a feature inside an application. It is an organisational unit. It can be assigned work, supervised, constrained, and evaluated. It does not wait for instructions at every step. It waits only for permission boundaries.

This is why the shift from tools to agents is irreversible.

Once an organisation allows work to be expressed as outcomes rather than instructions, the internal logic of work changes. Process maps lose relevance. Application boundaries blur. Responsibility migrates away from "who clicked" and toward "under what conditions was this allowed to run."

What appears at first as a productivity gain is, in reality, a governance event.

## Generative AI and Agents Feed Each Other

Generative AI and agents are often discussed as competing ideas. In practice, they are complementary.

Generative models structure meaning. They translate ambiguous human intent into machine-readable narratives: what a customer wants, what a transaction represents, what risk might be emerging, what explanation should be given.

Agents act on that meaning.

A generative model drafts the rationale.<br>
An agent evaluates confidence.<br>
Another agent checks constraints.<br>
A payment agent executes.

This is why leaders like Sam Altman and Demis Hassabis increasingly describe AI systems as entities that can plan, reason, and act over time. Their bias is not banking, but general intelligence. The implication for banks is direct: once meaning and action are linked, governance must move into the system itself.

## Agents Inside Financial Institutions Today

Banks may avoid the word *agent*, but their systems already behave like them.

At Visa, fraud prevention systems autonomously approve, decline, or challenge transactions in milliseconds using network-wide behavioural signals[73]. Humans do not approve individual decisions. They define thresholds, escalation logic, and override authority.

At Stripe, systems such as Radar do more than flag fraud[74]. They adapt behaviour in real time, adjusting thresholds and routing based on observed patterns. Stripe is explicit that these systems are designed to reduce human intervention, not assist it.

Inside large banks, the same logic appears quietly.

At JPMorgan Chase, internal treasury and liquidity systems rebalance intraday liquidity, trigger collateral movements, and intervene automatically when signals conflict[75]. Humans supervise limits and exceptions. They do not approve each action.

At Capital One, customer service systems increasingly resolve issues end to end: recognising intent, verifying identity through layered signals, reversing fees, executing account changes, and escalating only when confidence drops[76]. The human becomes the exception handler, not the default.

These are agents in every meaningful sense.
They observe, infer, act, escalate, and recover under constraints.

## Outside Banking, the Pattern Is Clear

Other industries adopted agents earlier because latency mattered more than explanation.

At Amazon, agentic systems reroute inventory, reprioritise fulfilment, and rebalance capacity continuously[77]. Humans design the rules of engagement. They do not approve each move.

In autonomous driving systems at Waymo and Tesla, agents continuously sense, infer, act, and override themselves when confidence drops. The ethical and legal question is not whether the car "decided", but whether the system was designed to fail safely.

In cybersecurity, firms such as CrowdStrike deploy agentic response systems that isolate endpoints, revoke credentials, and contain threats in milliseconds[78]. Human review comes later.

These examples demonstrate a consistent rule:

Agents appear first where execution speed and recoverability matter more than explanation.

Banking has now crossed that threshold.

## Customers Are Building Agents Too

The most disruptive aspect of agentic banking is not that banks are building agents.

It is that customers are building them as well, often without thinking of them as "financial".

When we say customers are building agents, we do not mean they are training models. They are authoring context. This is already obvious in gaming.

Platforms like Roblox allow millions of users to create autonomous scripts and non-player characters that manage in-game economies, negotiate trades, enforce rules, and respond dynamically to player behaviour[79]. What matters is not that these agents are playful. It is that users are already comfortable authoring behaviour and delegating decisions.

At Epic Games, the Fortnite Creative and UEFN ecosystems let creators design logic-driven agents that manage assets, trigger rewards, enforce scarcity, and respond to intent[80]. These are event-driven, rule-bound systems embedded in economic loops.

Model Context Protocols make this explicit. Using simple MCP-style connections, customers can already decide:

- which accounts an agent can see
- which transactions update in real time
- which alerts trigger action
- which messages, payments, or balances matter

This can be as basic as routing bank CSV exports into an AI tool, or as sophisticated as live aggregation across multiple institutions using Plaid, PayPal, Square, and messaging automation.

What matters is not the tooling.
It is the shift in control.

The bank no longer defines the customer's financial picture.
The customer does.

Agents do not need the bank's app to understand the customer. They need permissioned access to context.

This is how agency escapes interfaces.

In these environments, users already understand something banks struggle to articulate: agency is about control over rules, not control over every action.

The same pattern now appears in everyday apps.

On Discord, bots manage communities, assign roles, enforce policies, coordinate payments, and run marketplaces. Entire servers operate with agent-like systems acting as governors rather than assistants.

On Telegram, bots already initiate payments, manage subscriptions, run escrow, and interact with crypto wallets. In many emerging markets, Telegram bots already function as de facto financial agents.

Even WhatsApp, under Meta, is evolving toward agent-embedded commerce through WhatsApp Business APIs. Once generative AI is layered in, conversation becomes intention, and intention becomes execution.

Users are learning to delegate decisions long before banks finish debating them.

## The Balance-Sheet Consequence

Here I need to remind the reader that this is where agents stop being a product discussion and become a balance-sheet issue.

When agents route payments, assemble liquidity, hedge exposure, or escalate disputes automatically, balance-sheet exposure shifts in real time. Liquidity moves before committees meet. Credit is extended or withdrawn before reports are written. Errors become losses instantly.

This is why Chapter 3 insisted that the business is still determined on the balance sheet.

Agents do not change that.
They accelerate it.

A bank that allows agents to act without owning the orchestration layer will still hold regulated exposure while others determine when and how that exposure is triggered.

That is how banks become utilities.

## From APIs to Execution Partners

Banks still talk about partnerships as if they were in the API era.

In the digital age, partnerships meant integrations and distribution. The bank provided accounts and compliance. The partner provided engagement.

AI breaks this model.

In an agentic world, partnerships are no longer about interfaces. They are about shared execution surfaces.

The most important partners will not only be fintechs. They will be gaming ecosystems, logistics networks, retail platforms, cloud providers, and machine-to-machine payment systems where no human is present at all.

A real AI-age partnership is not an API contract. It is a system where agents can act across institutional boundaries, data and liquidity flow with consent, and control rules are mutually legible.

Banks that insist on owning the interface will lose relevance.
Banks that insist on owning decision constraints and execution rights will remain central.

## Agents Redefine Organisational Boundaries

The real challenge is not stopping agents from acting.

It is preventing them from acting outside institutional intent.

This is where the control layer of the AI stack becomes decisive.

Agents must operate within explicit boundaries: decision limits, confidence thresholds, escalation paths, kill authority, and fallback modes.

Without these, agents do not create efficiency. They create fragility.

This connects directly to ethics and cybersecurity: ethics lives in the valves, and security lives in the ability to stop execution.

Once agents operate across data, inference, control, and execution, organisational boundaries weaken.

Authority no longer maps cleanly to departments.
Risk no longer sits in one function.
Operations no longer happen "after" decisions.

The institution becomes a network of constrained agents, supervised continuously rather than directed episodically.

This is not decentralisation.
It is a different form of central control.

## Can AI Agents Become an AI Bank?

Is this even a question?

But bankers ask this question because they saw what the platform players wanted to do in the digital age.

The preliminary players in agentic commerce point to the same conclusion. Becoming a bank is not the prize.

The prize is to embed banking functions inside life, while letting regulated institutions absorb the risk.

Most platforms do not want balance sheets.
They want execution primitives.

In an AI world, being a bank is no longer defined by a licence alone.

It is defined by the ability to hold identity, manage risk, orchestrate trust, and execute value reliably.

This opens the field to cloud platforms, marketplaces, infrastructure providers, virtual economies, and data platforms that already intermediate behaviour and value.

In AI, banks will not be replaced by fintechs.
They will be replaced by coordination engines that perform banking functions.

Banks that understand agents as organisational units can compete.
Banks that treat agents as software features will not.

Banks that insist on being the destination will be bypassed.
Players that embed themselves as governed execution partners will remain indispensable.

And these do not even have to be banks.

Agents force banks to confront a final question: Who is accountable when a system acts?

Not when it recommends.
Not when it informs.
But when it moves money.

That question cannot be answered by technology teams.
It must be answered by the institution.

Peer-to-peer, BNPL, and agentic commerce all point to the same conclusion.

Becoming a bank is not the prize.

The prize is to embed banking functions inside life, while letting regulated institutions absorb the risk.

Most platforms did not want balance sheets.
They want execution primitives.

Banks that insist on being the destination will be bypassed.
Banks that embed themselves as governed execution partners will remain indispensable.

# CHAPTER NINE

# Risk, Regulation and Networked Belief

*"We were in too much of a hurry to notice what we were becoming"*
*– John Steinbeck*[81]

---

For most of modern banking history, risk was something you could locate.

It lived on the balance sheet.
It accumulated as exposure.
It could be measured, stress-tested, provisioned for, and absorbed.

That mental model shaped not only regulation, but how banks organised themselves internally. Risk lived in the second line. Models were validated periodically. Committees reviewed outcomes. The institution assumed that judgement, belief, and intention were human — and therefore slow.

That assumption no longer holds.

In the AI Bank, the most dangerous risks are not static exposures. They are manufactured beliefs and machine-mediated intentions that form, align, and execute faster than governance can react. Regulation struggles with this. But so does the bank itself.

This chapter is therefore about two failures happening at once: the failure of traditional risk management inside the bank, and the failure of traditional regulatory frameworks outside it.

They are related, but not identical.

## Risk was Labour Intensive

Before AI, risk management inside a bank rested on a workable division of labour.

The first line originated business and took risk.
The second line measured, constrained, and challenged it.
The third line audited the process.

Model risk management assumed stable models, explainable logic, periodic validation and bounded use cases.

Most importantly, it assumed that intent preceded action.

A human decided to lend.
A human decided to trade.
A human decided to override a model.

Systems executed what had already been judged.

Even when models were complex, belief formation remained human. Risk committees existed because there was time to convene them.

That world is disappearing.

The first place internal risk management breaks is not capital.
It is model governance.

Once AI systems adapt continuously, traditional validation cycles become ceremonial. A model that was "approved" six months ago may no longer behave like the model that is live today.

CROs already know this.

This is why many risk functions are quietly shifting away from:

- one-off model approval
- static documentation
- annual validation cycles

and toward:

- continuous monitoring
- drift detection
- behavioural analytics

But this creates a new problem.

Monitoring is not control.

Seeing that a model is drifting does not stop it from acting.

At the same time, I must add that quant investors like Cliff Asness have been blunt that better models do not eliminate uncertainty; they often concentrate it[82]. In finance, intelligence without humility tends to amplify risk rather than reduce it.

## From Risk as Exposure to Risk as Behaviour

Traditional risk frameworks assume that instability emerges from exposures.

Too much leverage. Too much duration. Too much concentration. Those risks still matter. But in an AI-mediated system, they are no longer the primary trigger.

Instability now emerges from behaviour.

Belief forms faster than fundamentals can be checked.
Signals propagate faster than committees can convene.
Actions are taken before narratives can be corrected.

This is not theoretical. It is already visible in markets, payments, and liquidity flows.

The collapse of Silicon Valley Bank was an early illustration, not because of its balance sheet, but because belief moved faster than governance. Depositors did not read financial statements. They reacted to networked conviction.

AI does not invent this dynamic.
It industrialises it.

## From Basel I to Basel III: Risk as Position

Regulators are not the enemy of the AI Bank. Uncontrolled intelligence is.

That distinction is already understood inside supervisory circles, even if it is still framed cautiously in public language. Across central banks, prudential regulators, and supervisory agencies, the conversation has moved decisively away from whether AI should be used in banking, and toward whether institutions can control behaviour when belief, decision, and execution collapse into a single loop.

For most of modern banking history, supervision rested on a shared assumption: judgement was human, belief was slow, and action could be paused.

AI breaks all three.

The Basel framework has always evolved in response to where risk appeared last. The following is the sequence I outlined in my previous book[83]:

**Basel I** emerged when the central concern was credit exposure. Balance sheets were expanding globally, and regulators needed a common language to ensure banks held sufficient capital against lending risk. Risk was something you could point to on the asset side of the balance sheet.

**Basel II** responded to complexity. As banks adopted internal models, securitisation expanded, and risk transfer became more sophisticated, regulators accepted that risk could no longer be standardised entirely. Model risk was internalised, but the underlying assumption remained: risk was still fundamentally a *position* that could be measured, validated, and reviewed.

**Basel III**, forged in the aftermath of the global financial crisis, acknowledged that this view was incomplete. Liquidity risk, leverage, and interconnectedness mattered as much as credit exposure. Stress did not wait politely on balance sheets. It propagated through funding markets, confidence channels, and correlated behaviour.

Basel III added buffers, liquidity coverage ratios, net stable funding ratios, and leverage constraints. It recognised that risk could migrate faster than capital absorbed it.

But even Basel III assumed something critical:
that governance would still operate at human speed.

Basel III was designed for a world in which:

- behaviour moved faster than capital, but
- still slower than governance.

AI breaks that balance.

Once decisions are automated, learning systems adapt continuously, and agents act on probabilistic belief, risk no longer migrates faster than governance — it outruns it.

Risk does not first appear as a deteriorating ratio.
It appears as behaviour in motion.
Payment flows surge.
Liquidity reroutes.

Limits are hit simultaneously across institutions.
Confidence hardens into executable belief.

By the time capital buffers are relevant, the damage is already systemic.

This is why the next regulatory regime — let's call it Basel V — is already forming, even if no one has named it yet.

## Basel V: Risk as Behaviour in Motion

Basel V will not be defined primarily by new ratios.

It will govern behaviour under speed.

Where previous frameworks focused on:

- exposure
- buffers
- positions

Basel V will most likely focus on:

- observability
- intervention authority
- behavioural containment
- stop-power at execution

This is not my speculation. It is already visible in how supervisors are questioning banks.

They are no longer satisfied with:

- model validation in isolation
- periodic reporting
- ex post explanations

They increasingly ask:

- Who owns model behaviour in production?
- What happens when multiple models drift together?

- Can automated decisions be slowed or segmented in real time?
- Who has the authority to stop execution when confidence breaks?

Capital absorbs losses.
Liquidity buys time.
Control prevents cascades.

That I believe is what the logic of Basel V will be. This is where the work of the Bank for International Settlements (BIS) becomes crucial. The BIS exists to see what national regulators cannot: systemic patterns across borders and institutions. Its bias is tempo, not innovation.

In its Annual Economic Reports (2023 and 2024), the BIS explicitly frames artificial intelligence and machine learning as amplifiers of speed and procyclicality[84]. The concern is not that AI will make banks reckless, but that it will make them synchronised.

When Agustín Carstens, former Governor of the Bank of Mexico and former General Manager of the BIS, speaks about AI and financial stability, his focus is consistently on timeliness[85]. Supervisory tools calibrated for quarterly or annual adjustment cannot cope with systems that reprice, reroute, and rebalance continuously.

The BIS is, in effect, describing the conditions that make Basel III insufficient.

What it has not yet named is the consequence: supervision must move from positions to flows.

The Financial Stability Board (FSB) approaches the same problem from a coordination lens. In its 2023 report on Artificial Intelligence and Financial Stability[86], the FSB highlights risks from:

- herding behaviour
- feedback loops
- common data and model dependencies
- third-party AI providers

The FSB's bias is cross-border alignment. When it labels AI risk as *systemic*, it is not worried about one bank failing. It is worried about many institutions behaving the same way at the same time.

This is Basel V logic, even if it is not called that. The FSB is describing risk as synchronised behaviour, not exposure.

The Bank of England, both as a central bank and a prudential supervisor, has been unusually candid about the limits of existing frameworks.

In its discussion papers on machine learning in UK financial services, the BoE acknowledges that adaptive models challenge core assumptions of model risk management: stability, explainability, and periodic review[87].

This concern was sharpened in speeches by Sir Jon Cunliffe, former Deputy Governor for Financial Stability, who repeatedly warned that automation pushes execution beyond the reach of traditional policy tools — particularly in payments and settlement systems[88].

The BoE is effectively saying that human-in-the-loop becomes post-mortem once execution accelerates.

That is a direct challenge to Basel III governance assumptions.

## The CRO's roles are already changing

Traditionally, intention was not treated as a risk variable.

Risk models assessed probability of default, loss given default, exposure at default. They did not assess why a decision was being made, only what decision was made.

AI changes this.

When intention is inferred probabilistically and executed automatically, intention itself becomes a risk object.

Two customers with identical balance sheets may be treated differently because models infer different future behaviours. Two treasury actions may be taken because models infer different confidence trajectories.

Risk managers are now confronted with a new question: *Do we agree with the intention this system has inferred?*

That question cannot be answered with a capital ratio.

This is why the role of the CRO (Chief Risk Officer) is quietly being rewritten.

The CRO can no longer act solely as a reviewer of outcomes. They are being pushed upstream, into the design of decision boundaries.

Increasingly, CROs are being asked to sign off on:

- confidence thresholds
- escalation triggers
- override authority
- kill switches
- behavioural segmentation logic

This is uncomfortable, because it collapses the distance between risk and business.

But it is unavoidable.

In an AI Bank, risk management is no longer about saying "no" after the fact. It is about designing how the system is allowed to say yes or no before the risk event actually happens.

## Manufactured Belief as a New Risk

This is the most under-appreciated risk in the AI Bank, largely because it has not happened yet.

AI does not merely respond to belief. It can manufacture it. What Basel frameworks have never had to contend with before is manufactured belief.

Generative AI amplifies narratives. Agentic AI acts on them. Together, they turn confidence into executable code. This is not captured by capital ratios. It is not visible in stress tests.

It shows up first in payments, liquidity routing, and market microstructure — exactly where Basel III is weakest.

Large language models, recommender systems, and agentic tools can:

- amplify narratives
- simulate consensus
- reinforce confidence signals
- suppress uncertainty

In financial networks, belief is not cosmetic. Belief moves money.

The Reddit-era market episodes of the 2020s were not anomalies. They were prototypes. Human coordination amplified by algorithms already demonstrated how quickly belief could detach from fundamentals.

AI turns this into infrastructure.

Bots argue with bots. Agents reinforce signals from other agents. Conviction becomes machine-generated, not socially negotiated.

From a banking perspective, this matters because:

- deposit confidence becomes programmable
- liquidity moves at the speed of narrative
- markets respond to simulated certainty, not verified truth

This is systemic risk in its new form.

Yoshua Bengio, one of the founders of modern deep learning, has warned repeatedly about emergent behaviour in networked, goal-driven systems[89]. His bias is structural. Once agents interact at scale, behaviour synchronises faster than humans can intervene.

## Human Discretion Repositioned

I would argue that regulatory insistence on "human-in-the-loop" is increasingly misplaced.

By the time a human reviews an AI-mediated decision, behaviour may already have propagated and execution already occurred. Supervisors understand that capital buffers cannot absorb belief cascades.

Once confidence breaks, liquidity moves before intervention tools can be deployed. Once narratives harden, explanations arrive too late.

This is why regulators are increasingly focused on:

- observability of automated decision pathways
- traceability of signal propagation
- intervention authority over execution, not advice

Supervision is no longer about reviewing outcomes. It is about constraining behavioural amplification.

In this environment, "human-in-the-loop" is a comforting fiction.

By the time a human reviews an AI-mediated decision, belief may already have propagated and action already taken.

In an AI Bank, human discretion moves upstream.

Humans design the envelope:

- what systems may optimise
- what signals they may amplify
- when speed must yield to friction
- when execution must be paused, throttled, or reversed

This is not abdication. It is the only form of responsibility that still works.

## Financial Inclusion and Network Risk

In financial inclusion markets, these dynamics become impossible to ignore.

This is where AI's promise and its danger collide most visibly.

In India, the Reserve Bank of India has actively encouraged the use of AI-driven credit assessment to expand access beyond traditional bureau data[90]. At the same time, it has insisted on explainability, auditability, and meaningful recourse for borrowers. The institutional bias is deliberate: inclusion matters, but inclusion without brakes becomes instability. Credit must scale, but judgement must remain contestable.

That posture reflects a hard-earned lesson. When AI is used to extend credit into previously excluded populations, errors do not remain isolated. They propagate through households, communities, and informal economies. What looks like a model optimisation at the portfolio level can become distress at the social level.

In parts of Africa, that lesson was learned the hard way.

Several digital lenders deployed AI-driven optimisation models that rapidly expanded small-ticket credit using behavioural data from mobile phones[91]. Defaults, rollovers, and penalty fees escalated just as quickly. By the time complaints surfaced, reputational damage was done and regulatory responses lagged behind reality. The systems did exactly what they were designed to do: maximise repayment probability and yield.

The failure was not malicious intent.
It was network amplification.

AI compressed decision cycles so tightly that harm scaled faster than governance, consumer protection, or social norms could respond. Borrowers were not evaluated as individuals over time; they were processed as signals inside a network. Once that network tipped, outcomes deteriorated everywhere at once.

These were not moral failures.
They were network failures.

In inclusion contexts, AI does not simply make better or worse decisions. It synchronises behaviour. And when synchronisation replaces judgement, small model errors turn into systemic outcomes.

That is why inclusion markets are the stress test for AI in banking. They reveal, earlier than developed markets, what happens when speed outruns recourse and optimisation outruns legitimacy.

## Risk as Legitimacy in the AI Bank

In the AI Bank, risk management is no longer primarily about avoiding loss.

It is about preserving legitimacy.

A bank that cannot explain its behaviour, slow its systems, or counteract manufactured belief will lose trust long before it breaches a capital ratio.

That is why risk, regulation, AI safety, and network theory now converge.

Not as separate disciplines. As a single design problem.

How should the AI Bank be built internally so that judgement, belief, and execution remain governable? That is where the real AI stack of the Bank and the operating model makes Basel V survivable.

# CHAPTER TEN

# Cybersecurity in the Age of Intelligence

*"The supreme art of war is to subdue the enemy without fighting."*
*– Sun Tzu*[92]

---

AI has turned cybersecurity from a technology problem into a coordination problem.

That shift is subtle, but decisive.

Attackers no longer need to outthink systems one target at a time. They scale horizontally. They write better phishing than humans. They automate reconnaissance. They generate deepfake instructions that feel real enough to override common sense and internal process. Deception no longer arrives as an anomaly. It arrives as something that *looks correct.*

Defenders can also scale.
But only if the institution is organised for it.

This is where most banks fall behind.

## When Identity Collapses

One of the clearest warnings was from Sam Altman, CEO of OpenAI, not as a cybersecurity specialist but as the person overseeing the deployment of the most capable generative models in the world. Altman has been unusually blunt in public discussions about AI-driven voice and video impersonation.

His warning is simple and devastating: in an AI world, a voice is no longer evidence.

This is no longer hypothetical.

In 2024, multiple multinational firms publicly disclosed losses after employees acted on what appeared to be video calls from senior executives that were later confirmed to be AI-generated deepfakes[93]. In one widely reported case in Hong Kong, a finance employee transferred tens of millions of dollars after participating in a video conference where every other "participant" was synthetic[94].

The trend is clear. Identity signals that were once expensive to fake are now cheap to generate. Banks have historically treated voiceprints, familiar speech patterns, and conversational nuance as a form of identity. Call-centre overrides, verbal confirmations, and "known customer" routines were built on the assumption that impersonation carried friction.

AI destroys that assumption.

The implication for the AI Bank is uncomfortable but unavoidable:

Authentication can no longer be something you *sound like.*
It must be something you can prove continuously.

Anything else is nostalgia disguised as control.

## Cyber Is No Longer a Perimeter

The modern bank's exposure is no longer confined to its own walls.

It extends through cloud dependencies, vendor ecosystems, APIs, open-banking integrations, and software supply chains. One misconfiguration becomes an open door. One overlooked alert becomes weeks of silent exfiltration. One supplier becomes a systemic vulnerability.

Recent incidents make this painfully clear.

The 2023 breach of MOVEit Transfer, a widely used managed file-transfer product, did not target banks directly[95]. It targeted *infrastructure*. Yet it exposed data across hundreds of organisations simultaneously, including financial institutions, regulators, and service providers.

The lesson was not about a single vulnerability.
It was about blast radius.

Similarly, repeated large-scale cloud outages at hyperscalers over the past two years have shown that availability risk is now tightly coupled with concentration risk. Banks were not breached, but they were effectively paralysed.

This is why leaders like Jen Easterly, Director of the US Cybersecurity and Infrastructure Security Agency (CISA), consistently frame cybersecurity as a collective resilience problem, not a tooling problem. Her bias is national-scale incident response: no single organisation ever sees the whole attack surface, and no single control prevents cascading failure.

Banks should recognise themselves in that description.

## Zero Trust Architecture Meets Reality

Many banks now describe themselves as "zero trust" organisations.

Few operate that way under stress.

John Kindervag, who originally defined Zero Trust architecture, was explicit that it was never meant to be a product[96]. It was meant to be an operating discipline: *never trust, always verify*. Over time, the term was diluted into marketing language.

Recent breaches show the cost of that dilution.

In multiple ransomware incidents affecting financial and non-financial firms alike, attackers did not "break in" at the perimeter. They moved laterally through trusted connections, exploiting over-permissioned service accounts and implicit trust between systems.

In an AI Bank, zero trust cannot be rhetorical.

It must mean that:

- third-party and vendor risk is audited continuously, not annually
- cloud misconfiguration is treated as a first-line control failure, not an IT detail
- identity and access are enforced dynamically, not statically
- telemetry is unified across systems, not reviewed in silos

Institutions like Capital One, which adopted cloud-native architectures early, learned this lesson publicly. Their response was not to retreat from the cloud, but to rebuild security around continuous control validation. The trend is clear: speed without discipline multiplies blast radius.

## Vendor Concentration

This is where cybersecurity and financial stability converge.

Banks are now deeply concentrated on a small number of hyperscalers, identity providers, and cybersecurity vendors. When these platforms fail, the question is no longer whether the bank was "hacked". It is whether the bank can operate at all.

The trend regulators are now watching is not breach frequency, but shared dependency risk.

A single vulnerability in a common vendor can create simultaneous exposure across dozens of systemically important institutions.

This is not a tail risk. It is an architectural feature of modern banking.

A serious AI Bank plans for hyperscaler and critical-vendor failure the way it plans for liquidity stress: as a scenario, not an exception.

Incident response is rehearsed like a fire drill, not documented like a policy.

Because in a world of shared infrastructure, resilience is not about avoiding failure. It is about failing without cascading.

## Protocol Risk Becomes Operational Risk

As finance becomes more programmable, failure modes become composable.

A smart-contract exploit is no longer just a technical bug. It becomes a liquidity event.
A bridge failure becomes a settlement crisis.
A stablecoin de-peg becomes a collateral shock.

The collapses and near-collapses of algorithmic stablecoins and DeFi bridges over the past few years illustrate this vividly. What looked like isolated protocol failures rapidly became market-wide stress events once automation amplified them.

AI accelerates this dynamic.

Agentic systems can route, leverage, and rebalance at machine speed. Contagion no longer waits for headlines. It propagates through automation.

This is why serious banks increasingly treat DeFi-facing exposure as operational resilience, not ideology.

If you cannot map dependencies, you cannot price them.
If you cannot observe flows, you cannot contain incidents.
If you cannot slow the system, you cannot claim control.

## From Preventing Fraud to Surviving Deception

Traditional cybersecurity assumed fraud had intent that could be detected.

AI breaks this assumption.

In a networked, AI-mediated system, the dominant threat is not fraud. It is deception without explicit intent. Signals are valid. Transactions are authorised. Behaviour is syntactically correct. Outcomes are still harmful.

This is the symmetry of deception:

All parties share accurate information,

while motives remain opaque.

AI cannot reliably "detect" deception, because deception no longer violates rules. It exploits them.

This is why thinkers like Bruce Schneier, one of the most influential security technologists of the past three decades, have long argued that security emerges from systems, not controls. Schneier's bias is architectural: no classifier outperforms adversaries at scale. Only system-level resilience does.

Recent incidents bear this out. Many breaches were detected quickly. What failed was not detection, but coordination.

## Cybersecurity as a Learning System

The only viable defence in an AI Bank is not stronger perimeters or smarter models.

It is participatory verification.

More observers.
More redundancy.

Faster collective response.

Cybersecurity becomes a learning system, not a gatekeeping one. Safety emerges from diversity, scale, and rapid adaptation, not from the illusion of perfect prevention.

This is why high-reliability organisations treat cyber near-misses the way aviation treats safety incidents: as signals to adapt, not failures to conceal.

## What AI Banks Must Do Differently

Most banks still approach AI security defensively: "How do we protect our models?"

The better question is structural: "How do we ensure our institution can still coordinate when deception is cheap and scale is free?"

That requires:

- collapsing silos between security, risk, data, and operations
- treating cyber as a production system, not a compliance function
- designing for observability and interruption, not just prevention
- assuming synthetic adversaries by default
- rehearsing failure as a governance capability

Cybersecurity in the AI Bank is not a cost centre.
It is a condition of legitimacy.

A pattern should now be unmistakable.

- Payments are the first stress point.
- Belief and intention are manufactured.
- Risk moves faster than governance.
- Cyber incidents reveal coordination failure, not tool failure.

Cybersecurity is not separate from this story.
It is where all of it becomes visible.

Our attention should be on the operating model of the AI Bank, because none of these controls matter unless the organisation itself is designed to act on them. That is where power finally becomes explicit.

Cybersecurity in an AI bank becomes a learning system, not a gatekeeping one. Safety emerges from scale, diversity, and rapid adaptation, not from control.

# CHAPTER ELEVEN

# Ethics is in the Plumbing

*In theory, theory and practice are the same. In practice, they are not."*
*– Yogi Berra*[97]

---

AI does not create unethical banks. It exposes them.

For most of modern banking history, ethics lived at the surface. It appeared in codes of conduct, policy manuals, and committees that reviewed decisions after they were made. When something failed, institutions asked whether rules had been broken or intent had been flawed.

That framing no longer works.

In an AI Bank, ethics is not about intent at the moment of decision. It is about behaviour under pressure. Every automated decision embeds values. Every optimisation encodes trade-offs. Every model reflects assumptions about fairness, risk, and legitimacy, whether anyone explicitly designed them or not.

This is why ethics in an AI Bank does not sit in mission statements or training slides.

It sits in the plumbing.

Plumbing determines where pressure builds, how flows are routed, where valves close automatically, and what happens when the system is stressed. When it works, no one notices. When it fails, damage spreads silently and quickly, often far from the original fault.

AI ethics behaves the same way. It determines who absorbs pressure, who is cut off first, and which failures propagate before humans can react.

The ethical fault-lines of AI in banking are therefore not abstract. They are operational, systemic, and already visible.

## From Principles to Power

The modern ethics debate did not start in banks. It started with scientists warning that scale and opacity would turn small distortions into structural harm.

In the paper *"On the Dangers of Stochastic Parrots"*[98], Emily M. Bender and Timnit Gebru argued that large AI systems inevitably embed bias and discrimination because they absorb the world as it was, not as institutions wish it had been. Their warning was not ideological. It was architectural: when systems are trained without contextual limits, bias becomes a feature, not a bug.

Joy Buolamwini, founder of the Algorithmic Justice League, made this tangible by showing how algorithmic errors disproportionately affected darker-skinned individuals[99]. Her insight maps directly to finance: when AI errors scale, unequal error distribution becomes inevitable unless it is actively countered.

Privacy advocates pushed the critique further.

Meredith Whittaker, now President of the Signal Foundation, has argued that modern AI systems are born from surveillance incentives[100]. In banking terms, this reframes the debate about surveillance, privacy and consent. When personalisation, fraud prevention, and risk management all rely on continuous data extraction, ethics is no longer about whether data can be collected, but whether its use remains legitimate.

Even security thinkers converge on the same concern. Bruce Schneier has long argued that security failures are rarely technical; they are systemic. In banking, ethics fails the same way: not because a rule was broken, but because the system behaved exactly as designed under stress.

## Bias and Discrimination

AI systems learn from historical data. That data reflects past discrimination, unequal access, and systemic exclusion. In a human system, bias could be episodic and contested. In an automated system, bias and discrimination become persistent and scalable.

In banking, this surfaces repeatedly in credit approval and pricing, fraud and AML false positives, financial inclusion and exclusion, and product suitability. The ethical risk here is rarely malicious intent. It is automated repetition of historical unfairness at machine speed.

Several banks have faced regulatory scrutiny and litigation after AI-driven credit models produced systematically worse outcomes for women, minorities, or first-time borrowers, even when financial profiles were similar. In many cases, the institution could not meaningfully explain *why* the model behaved that way.

Ethics therefore requires counter-pressure built into the system itself: outcome testing rather than model assurances, bias monitoring rather than bias statements, and override authority when fairness drifts.

Without these controls, the system behaves exactly as designed, and ethics becomes a post-incident explanation rather than a preventative mechanism.

## Explainability Is a Moral Boundary

One of the most persistent tensions in AI is explainability versus performance.

The most powerful models are often the least interpretable. In many industries, this trade-off is tolerated. In banking, it is not.

Regulators do not ask whether a model is accurate.
They ask whether a decision can be explained, challenged, and reversed.

The Consumer Financial Protection Bureau has been explicit: adverse-action obligations apply regardless of whether a decision was made by a neural network or a loan officer. "We can't explain it" is not an answer. It is a governance failure.

Ethics here is not transparency theatre.
It is contestability.

If a customer cannot understand why a decision was made, and if a human cannot meaningfully intervene when the outcome is wrong or harmful, the system is unethical — even if it is statistically optimal.

This is where explainability versus performance stops being a technical debate and becomes a moral boundary. Judgement that cannot be contested cannot be owned. Judgement that cannot be owned cannot be legitimate.

## Surveillance, Privacy and Consent are Design Questions

AI thrives on granular, continuous data. This creates persistent tension between personalisation and intrusion, fraud prevention and surveillance, insight and over-collection.

The ethical question is not "can we see this?"
It is "should we act on it?"

Banks increasingly operate systems that know where customers spend, when they travel, who they transact with, and how their behaviour shifts under stress. Without clear limits, surveillance, privacy and consent collapse into a single power asymmetry.

Consent that cannot be withdrawn is not consent. Monitoring that exceeds customer understanding becomes intrusion.

An AI Bank that accumulates omniscience without legitimacy will not retain trust. Ethics here must be enforced through hard design constraints: purpose-bound data use, proportionality, and revocable consent.

## Automation Bias and Abdicated Responsibility

Ethical failure is not only about models. It is also about people.

Humans tend to defer to machine outputs, especially under time pressure. This automation bias leads directly to abdicated responsibility.

Rubber-stamped approvals.
Ignored warnings.
Delayed intervention.
"The model did it" explanations.

AI does not remove responsibility.
It concentrates it.

Ethical AI therefore requires named ownership: who owns model behaviour, who owns overrides, who owns failures. Where responsibility diffuses, ethics leaks out of the system through the same pathways that accelerate decision-making.

## Manipulation and Behaviour Steering

AI systems do not just predict behaviour. They shape it.

This is where manipulation and behavioural steering become ethical fault-lines.

In banking, AI-driven nudging affects spending behaviour, risk appetite, product uptake, and investment decisions. The ethical line is crossed when customers are steered without awareness or when optimisation benefits the institution at the customer's expense.

Banking has always influenced behaviour. What changes in the AI era is opacity and scale. Ethics demands alignment, not exploitation — particularly as decisions are increasingly negotiated by agents rather than humans.

## Unequal Error Distribution Reveals Who Ethics Serves

AI errors do not affect everyone equally. This is the problem of unequal error distribution.

In banking, mistakes disproportionately harm low-income customers, small businesses, first-time borrowers, minorities, and those least able to navigate appeal processes.

An ethical AI Bank does not stop at aggregate accuracy metrics. It measures who bears the cost of being wrong and who benefits from optimisation.

Fairness is not about averages.
It is about impact.

Where errors land repeatedly on the same groups, ethics has already failed, regardless of model performance.

## Speed Without Due Process Is the New Ethical Failure Mode

AI collapses time.

In banking, this creates speed without due process: instant account freezes, automated de-risking, liquidity denial without recourse.

Processes that once involved review, explanation, and appeal now execute immediately. Ethics at machine speed therefore requires friction by design: cooling-off periods, escalation thresholds, and human interruptibility.

Justice does not disappear because systems move faster.

Due process must be redesigned to survive acceleration, especially at the execution and payment layers where decisions become irreversible.

## Model Bias, Drift, and Silent Value Change

AI systems evolve over time. This introduces model bias not just at deployment, but through drift.

Credit standards shift invisibly.
Risk appetite drifts.
Customer treatment changes without notice.

Ethical governance cannot rely on one-time approval. It requires continuous behavioural monitoring precisely because learning continues even when no one is watching.

Silent drift is the most dangerous plumbing failure of all. Pressure changes gradually, unnoticed, until rupture makes it visible.

## Ethics as Infrastructure

Taken together, these fault-lines lead to a simple conclusion.

Ethics in an AI Bank is not a committee.
It is not a policy.
It is not a slogan.

It is monitoring, escalation, intervention, and accountability.

Ethics must be engineered into production systems, because values that are not enforced in code do not survive scale.

In an AI Bank, ethics is not a constraint on innovation.
It is the condition for legitimacy.

Once ethics moves into the plumbing, authority can no longer hide at the surface. If systems act automatically, someone must decide where the valves sit, who can shut them, and under what conditions flow is allowed to continue.

Ethics defines what should not happen.
Leadership defines who is responsible when it almost does.

That is why the next question is no longer whether machines can decide.

It is who owns the judgement when they do.

# CHAPTER TWELVE

# Leadership When Machines Decide

*"I didn't invent the hydrogen bomb. I made it work."*
*Richard Garwin, when asked if he regretted inventing the hydrogen bomb*[101]

---

Up to this point in this book, the discussion has sounded familiar. Platforms. Use cases. Productivity. Talent. Vendors. Timelines. The language of transformation — but still recognisably the language of technology programmes.

Then someone asks a different kind of question.

Who owns a model's behaviour?
Who is accountable when a system does the "right" thing according to its training, but the wrong thing according to customers, regulators, or society?
Who has the authority to slow or stop execution when everything is working exactly as designed?

These are not implementation details.
They are questions of power.

AI does not simply change how work is done. It changes how judgement is exercised, how responsibility is distributed, and how legitimacy is maintained when action becomes continuous rather than episodic.

In an AI Bank, leadership is defined by who owns judgement when no single human makes the decision.

## When Leadership Becomes Explicit

The elevation of someone like Professor Manuela Veloso into the senior leadership at JPMorgan Chase was instructive precisely because it made ownership explicit. She is at the time of writing, the head of AI Research at the bank[102].

AI was not treated as an IT experiment or an innovation sideline. It was treated as a core business capability, with executive accountability.

This distinction matters.

As Teresa Heitsenrether has reinforced publicly, the priority was not experimentation first and governance later, but scaling AI inside the firm with controls designed in from the start[103].

That is a leadership choice, not a technology one.

Model behaviour is institutional behaviour.
If leadership does not own it, no one does.

## What Boards Are Really Asking

Boards rarely ask these questions directly. Instead, they surface in more comfortable forms.

Do we need an AI strategy?
Should we double down on digital?
Is this just another technology cycle?

These questions are understandable.
They are also evasive.

They reflect a desire to place AI inside an existing mental model, where technology arrives as a programme, is funded as a project, and is governed as an implementation risk.

AI does not fit that model.

This is where the conversation needs its first reset.

## The First Reframe: AI Is Not a Project Line Item

"How much should we invest in AI?"

This is the most common boardroom question. It sounds practical. It feels disciplined. It is also the wrong question — or more precisely, a question inherited from the digital banking era.

Boards ask it because they are used to treating technology as a capital project. Core banking replacements. CRM rollouts. Cloud migrations. These were finite programmes with defined end states.

AI is not.

AI behaves less like software and more like institutional capability. It has no end state. It compounds. It reshapes how decisions are made long after the initial deployment is forgotten.

The relevant comparison is not how much the bank spent on digital.

It is how much of the institution's judgement the bank intends to redesign.

That question immediately changes the tone of the room.

It forces leaders to confront not budgets, but authority.
Not timelines, but accountability.
Not speed, but control.

As David Solomon, CEO of Goldman Sachs has acknowledged in public discussions on AI, the hardest part of adoption is not experimentation[104]. It is clarity about where decision authority actually sits when machines are involved.

That clarity is still missing in many institutions.

## Should We Abandon Digital Banking?

At this point, another question usually surfaces — sometimes explicitly, sometimes only in the pause that follows.

Does this mean digital banking is over?

No.

Digital banking is not something you abandon.
It is something you finish.

Digital banking modernised channels, workflows, and cost structures. It cleaned up data pipelines. It forced real-time thinking. It built the operational foundations that AI now depends on. Without those foundations, AI cannot be deployed safely at scale.

But digital banking is also a trap if it is treated as the destination.

Digital was about interfaces, engagement, and unit economics.
AI is about where decisions are formed, constrained, and executed — often at machine speed, often through payments.

Digital banking made banks faster.
AI banking determines who controls the speed.

You do not abandon digital banking.
You stop pretending it is enough.

This applies equally to incumbents and digital-only banks.

Incumbents often underestimate how deeply AI challenges their governance structures. Digital banks often underestimate how deeply AI challenges their strategy. Incumbents layer AI onto committee-driven decision logic that cannot operate at machine speed. Digital banks automate experience while leaving judgement unchanged.

Different paths.

Same destination.

Loss of control.

## Leadership Roles Under Pressure

Traditional banking leadership evolved in a world where humans decided and systems executed. Digital banking accelerated execution, but it preserved that logic.

AI breaks it.

When judgement is embedded in models and execution becomes continuous, authority must be explicit. If it is not, responsibility fragments while risk concentrates.

This is why leadership roles are being reshaped.

The CIO moves from infrastructure stability toward orchestration — making hard trade-offs about where to build, where to buy, and where control must never be outsourced.

The CRO can no longer treat model risk as a specialist concern. Model behaviour becomes first-line risk, because behaviour now moves the balance sheet continuously.

The COO inherits the operational reality of agents acting across workflows, time zones, and institutional boundaries.

And the CEO faces the defining choice: whether the institution will own its judgement, or quietly outsource it.

There is no neutral position.

As Jamie Dimon, CEO of JP Morgan, has often remarked in a different context, complexity does not reduce accountability[105]. It concentrates it. AI simply makes that concentration visible.

## The Second Reframe: Invest in Decision Surfaces, Not Scale

Once boards accept that AI is not a project, the instinct is to scale.

Enterprise licences.
Horizontal copilots.
Bank-wide rollouts that feel safe because they look incremental.

This is the second mistake.

Early AI investment should not be biased toward scale. It should be biased toward decision surfaces.

Decision surfaces are points where judgement materially affects outcomes: credit approval and limit setting, fraud intervention thresholds, liquidity allocation and funding decisions, customer suitability and escalation logic, exception handling in operations.

These are the places where AI creates real leverage.
They are also the places where failure creates institutional risk.

Investing here forces the bank to confront governance, accountability, and explainability early, while mistakes are still survivable. Horizontal tooling creates activity. Decision surfaces create learning.

This is why productivity-first narratives are so dangerous.

James Gorman, chairman emeritus of Morgan Stanley, has warned that AI-driven workforce restructuring is inevitable. He is probably right. Productivity will rise. Roles will change.

But productivity that outpaces accountability is not efficiency.
It is accelerated institutional risk.

The fastest way to scale mistakes is to automate before authority, escalation, and intervention are explicit.

Governance cannot follow adoption.
It must lead it.

## A Board Heuristic for the AI Bank

At this point, boards need something more concrete than principles.

Rather than approving a single AI budget number, leadership should be required to answer four questions clearly and precisely, every year.

What percentage of our material decisions are now machine-supported?
Where do we lack kill authority, observability, or escalation clarity?
Which AI systems could move the balance sheet before humans convene?
What would we struggle to explain to a regulator in real time today?

These are not technical questions.
They are governance questions.

A bank that cannot answer them does not yet know how much it should invest, because it does not yet know what it is redesigning.

## The Final Reframe: AI Spend Is a Statement of Intent

In the end, AI investment is not about keeping up with peers.

It is a declaration of what kind of institution the bank intends to be.

A bank that invests minimally is choosing to remain reactive, providing balance-sheet capacity while others control intelligence.

A bank that invests aggressively without redesign is choosing speed over legitimacy.

The AI Bank invests deliberately.

Early in judgement.
Heavily in governance.

Continuously in learning.
Unapologetically in the ability to intervene.

As Larry Fink, co-founder and chairman of Blackrock has repeatedly argued in the context of risk and stewardship, under-investing in control functions rarely ends well[106]. AI governance belongs squarely in that category. It may not generate revenue directly, but it determines whether revenue is earned legitimately.

That is not an IT budget. It is an institutional choice.

One additional signal should give boards pause.

The system described earlier was not built over years by a large engineering organisation. It was assembled in roughly two weeks — using the same agentic tooling it ultimately exposed.

This is not a curiosity. It is a warning.

When AI systems can build production-grade AI systems, institutional time collapses. The constraint is no longer engineering capacity, vendor selection, or delivery methodology. It is governance readiness.

In such an environment, leadership cannot assume that adoption will be gradual, controllable, or synchronised with policy cycles. Capability will appear before permission. Execution will become possible before accountability is fully articulated.

This is why AI cannot be governed as a roadmap.

The question for leadership is no longer whether the institution will deploy agentic systems. That outcome is already determined by competitive pressure and organisational fatigue with manual coordination.

The real question is whether leadership will design authority, stop-power, and accountability *before* those systems become embedded into critical decision paths.

Once agents can act, restraint becomes a leadership decision, not a technical one.

# CHAPTER THIRTEEN

# Conclusion: A First Day at an AI Bank (2030)

*"In preparing for battle I have always found that plans are useless, but planning is indispensable."*
*– Dwight D. Eisenhower*[107]

---

If a bank intends to call itself an AI Bank, it must stop asking whether artificial intelligence is a programme, a tool, or an efficiency lever. Those were digital-era questions, born in a time when software accelerated execution without fundamentally altering responsibility.

The question that now matters is more exacting and more consequential: will this institution own its judgement, or will it merely host it? Will it govern belief, constrain intention, and retain stop-power at the precise moment execution occurs?

Designing deliberately is no longer optional. Systems that are not designed will still exist, but they will be inherited, opaque, and eventually uncontrollable.

Now imagine a member of Generation Alpha arriving for their first day in banking in 2030.

They do not walk into a marble lobby, nor are they assigned a desk, a branch, or a book of clients. There is no orientation speech about transformation, no ceremonial language about the future of finance. They may not even be physically present in an office. Instead, they log into a system.

What appears is not an organisational chart but a living map of decisions: active agents, running models, risk envelopes, escalation paths, and clearly defined intervention rights. The bank introduces itself not as a place, but as a governed intelligence. No one needs to explain what AI means for their role, because it is already visible in motion. Payments settle continuously. Credit reprices dynamically. Liquidity rebalances across the system. Fraud is intercepted before it crystallises into loss. When stress emerges, it does not arrive as a report or a meeting invitation; it surfaces first in flows.

Most execution occurs without human involvement. There is no reassurance that AI will "help" or "free people for higher-value work". Those arguments were resolved long before this graduate arrived. The question that matters now is narrower, and far more revealing: which decisions are you trusted to supervise?

On their first day, they are not assigned to a department. They are assigned to a decision surface — a credit boundary, a fraud escalation band, a liquidity throttle, or a behavioural-risk corridor. Their authority is defined precisely by what they are permitted to slow, override, or stop. This is how work is explained in an AI Bank.

The institution still employs people, but not as it once did. There are fewer processors, fewer routine decision-makers, and far fewer roles devoted to moving information between systems. Instead, the bank is populated by supervisors of behaviour, designers of constraints, translators between policy and code, and governors of machine judgement.

Some of these individuals are employees. Many are not. Specialists move in and out of the institution to stress-test models, audit behaviour, redesign control boundaries, or translate new regulatory requirements into executable rules. Some carry standing authority to intervene without ever appearing on an organisation chart. Others are engaged only when volatility rises or confidence fractures. What matters is no longer employment status, but who is permitted to intervene, in which decisions, and under what conditions.

The institution endures. Its perimeter does not.

Career progression no longer resembles a ladder. There are no predictable steps, no guaranteed titles, and no automatic accumulation of power. Progress is measured instead by the scope of decisions one has supervised, the severity of scenarios navigated, the quality of judgement exercised under stress, and the trust earned from both regulators and peers. The most senior figures are not those who authorised the most growth, but those who stopped the system at exactly the right moment. Reputation is built not on volume delivered, but on crises contained.

From the inside, the AI Bank does not feel flat, nor does it feel conventionally hierarchical. It feels bounded. Everyone understands what they may act upon, what must be escalated, and what is forbidden entirely. Authority is explicit because ambiguity is dangerous. Although the institution moves quickly, it is not optimised for speed. It is optimised for recoverability.

No one reassures this generation that AI will not replace them. That would be dishonest. Instead, the institution communicates something more durable without ever stating it explicitly: execution is cheap, judgement is scarce, and accountability is priceless. Those seeking safety will not find it here. Those seeking agency will.

Most days inside the AI Bank are uneventful, by design. The system is engineered so that nothing dramatic happens unless something is genuinely wrong. When it is, humans do not assemble afterward to explain decisions. They intervene in real time, within clearly defined authority. The institution does not celebrate automation. It celebrates containment.

Yet the most important feature of the AI Bank in 2030 is not visible from within.

It is experienced by customers as absence, punctuated by precision.

Customers do not manage money. They live their lives. Finance attaches itself quietly to what they are already doing, activating only when intent appears. Liquidity arrives when a payment would otherwise fail. Credit is extended at the moment commitment is required. Risk is hedged before exposure is felt. Fraud is avoided rather than explained. Most of the time, nothing happens — and that is success.

Invisibility, however, does not imply interchangeability. The customer may not know which institution acted on their behalf, but their agent does. In an AI-mediated world, preference is not stored in memory or sentiment; it is learned by systems. Customer agents remember which institutions execute reliably, which price fairly under stress, which reverse mistakes cleanly, and which respect constraints rather than gaming them.

This is how banks remain institutions of choice — not through brand recall, engagement metrics, or sales calls, but by being selected again and again at moments of need.

The AI Bank no longer competes for attention. It competes for alignment. When a customer's agent detects intent — to buy, to invest, to protect, to commit — it seeks institutional agents whose rules, constraints, and execution histories align with that intent. Products are not pushed. They are assembled in real time, negotiated between agents, and applied precisely where action is required. A payment triggers credit. A transaction triggers insurance. A commitment triggers liquidity. The sale occurs as execution.

From the customer's perspective, this feels natural, almost invisible. From the bank's perspective, it is intensely competitive. Preference is earned transaction by transaction, exception by exception, reversal by reversal. The relationship the AI Bank seeks is not emotional. It is situational.

The institution aims to be present only at the moment its balance sheet is useful, and absent the rest of the time. To intervene without intruding. To enable without interrupting. To act without demanding attention. Trust is built not through what customers remember, but through what never goes wrong.

Behind this quiet experience sits an institution working harder than ever: supervising agents, constraining models, absorbing volatility, and defending legitimacy at machine speed. Customers should not see this work. Ethics is not announced; it is enforced in the valves and thresholds of the system.

This is the final inversion of the AI Bank. Internally, judgement becomes explicit, contested, and accountable in ways banking has never experienced before. Externally, finance dissolves into the background of everyday life, surfacing only when intent demands action.

The Gen Alpha banker logs in each day to decide what is allowed to happen.

The Gen Alpha customer logs in to nothing at all.

Both experiences depend on the same discipline: a bank that knows when to act, and when not to speak.

This book was never about whether banks would adopt artificial intelligence. That outcome was decided before it was written. It has been about whether banks understand how power must behave when execution is automated, when customers no longer need to be involved, and when preference is encoded into agent relationships rather than human memory.

Banking has always been the organised expression of power over money. In the AI era, that power finally learns restraint. And in an agentic world, being chosen quietly is the highest form of validation.

That is the AI Bank.

# Glossary

The following are keywords used in this book explained as simply as possible for the non-technical reader, as well as examples.

**Agent**

A piece of software that can observe, decide, and act instead of waiting for a human to click a button.
An app shows you your balance. An agent notices your rent is due tomorrow, sees you're short, moves money from savings, and pays the rent automatically.

**Agent Architecture**

The structural design that determines how AI agents are built, governed, connected, and deployed within an institution. It defines how they share information, escalate decisions, and remain controllable.
A bank may design agents so that a payment agent can act independently up to $1,000, but must escalate larger transfers to a supervisory agent before execution.

**Agentic AI**

AI systems that can perceive situations, reason about them, make decisions, and take actions autonomously over time, with limited human intervention.
A chatbot answers: "Your bill is $500."
An agentic AI notices the bill, checks your cash flow, negotiates a payment plan, schedules payments, and pauses if your income drops.

**AI-Native**

An organisation designed from the beginning assuming AI will participate in decisions, not just assist humans.
A digital bank adds AI to review applications faster.
An AI-native bank designs credit, fraud, and payments assuming machines will act first and humans will supervise.

**Artificial Intelligence (AI)**

Software that can learn from data, recognise patterns, and make predictions or decisions instead of following fixed rules.
A traditional system says: "If income is above X, approve the loan."
AI says: "People with this income, spending pattern, job history, and recent behaviour usually repay, so approve it now."

**Automation Bias**

The tendency for humans to trust machine decisions too much, especially when things are moving fast.
A staff member thinks, "The system approved it, so it must be fine," even when something feels wrong.

**Belief (Machine Belief)**

A probability-based judgement formed by AI about what is likely to happen.
The system believes there's an 85% chance you'll repay the loan. That belief, not certainty, drives the decision.

**Behavioural Risk**

Risk caused by how people or systems behave, especially when many react the same way at once.
Thousands of customers withdraw money at the same time because they believe something is wrong, even if the bank is solvent.

**Context**

Everything the AI system is allowed to see: data, permissions, history, and environment.
An AI that sees only your bank account behaves very differently from one that also sees your salary, bills, calendar, and recent travel.

**Context Architecture**

The intentional design of what information flows into AI, how often, and under what rules.
Allowing AI to see your spending but not your medical history is a context design choice.

**Control Layer**

The part of the system that decides what AI is allowed to do, when it must ask for help, and when it must stop.
AI may approve payments under $1,000, but anything above that requires human confirmation.

**Data Loss Prevention (DLP)**

Security tools and policies designed to prevent sensitive data from being accessed, shared, or leaked outside authorised channels.
A DLP system blocks an employee from emailing customer account data to a personal address.

**Decision Boundary**

A clear line defining when AI can act alone and when humans must intervene.
AI can freeze a suspicious card instantly, but only humans can close the account permanently.

**Decision Surface**

A moment where a decision directly changes outcomes.
Approving a loan, blocking a payment, or rerouting liquidity are all decision surfaces.

**Delegated Judgement**

Letting machines make or execute decisions on behalf of humans, within limits.
You allow your email spam filter to decide what you never see, without reviewing each message.

**Drift (Model Drift)**

When an AI system's behaviour slowly changes over time without anyone explicitly changing it.
A credit model gradually becomes stricter because the economy worsens, even though no rule was changed.

**Execution**

The moment when a decision becomes real and irreversible.
Approving a loan is a decision.
Sending the money is execution.

**Execution Environment**

The system where actions actually happen.
Payments systems are execution environments because once money moves, it's hard to undo.

**Explainability**

The ability to explain why a decision was made in a way a human can understand and challenge.
"It was declined because income is unstable," not "the model said no."

**Generative AI**

AI that creates content like text, images, or code.
ChatGPT writing a loan summary or explaining an investment strategy.

### Governance (AI Governance)

Who owns decisions, who is accountable, and who can stop the system when needed.
Knowing exactly who can shut down automated lending during a crisis.

### Human-in-the-Loop

A setup where humans review AI decisions.
A fraud system flags transactions, and staff review them.
In fast systems, this often happens after money has already moved.

### Inference

How AI draws conclusions from data.
Inferring that a customer is under financial stress based on spending patterns.

### Kill Switch

An emergency stop that immediately halts AI actions.
Stopping all automated payments during a cyberattack.

### KPIs (Key Performance Indicators)

Measurable values that indicate how effectively an individual, team, or organisation is achieving specific objectives.
A bank tracking the percentage of fraud detected automatically without customer complaints is using a KPI to measure AI effectiveness.

### LLM (Large Language Model)

An advanced AI system trained on massive amounts of text to understand and generate human language.
An LLM can draft a compliance report, summarise a loan agreement, or answer customer queries in natural language.

**Machine-Readable Trust**

Trust expressed in rules and permissions that machines can verify automatically.
An agent proves it is authorised to move money up to a certain amount for a specific purpose.

**Manufactured Belief**

Belief created or amplified by AI systems themselves.
Bots reinforcing each other's signals until markets panic without new information.

**Model**

The trained brain of an AI system.
A credit-scoring model trained on millions of past loans.

**Model Context Protocol (MCP)**

A standard that allows users or systems to define what context an AI can access and what tools it can use.
You allow your AI to access your calendar and bank account but not your emails.

**Observability**

The ability to see what the system is doing as it happens.
Watching live payment flows instead of reading reports days later.

**Orchestration**

The coordination and management of multiple AI agents, systems, and workflows to achieve a defined outcome.
An orchestration layer connects credit assessment, fraud checks, compliance screening, and payment execution into one seamless process.

**Orchestration Layer**

The layer that coordinates multiple systems and tools.
An AI that connects banking, shopping, insurance, and logistics into one workflow.

**Permissioned vs Permissionless**

Permissioned systems restrict who can join; permissionless systems let anyone participate.
A private bank network versus a public blockchain.

**Probabilistic System**

A system that works in likelihoods, not certainties.
"There is a 70% chance this transaction is fraud," not "this is fraud."

**Product Development Lifecycle (PDLC)**

The structured process of creating a new product, from idea and prototype through launch and ongoing improvement.
A bank designing a new AI-powered savings tool would test it internally, pilot it with customers, launch it, then continuously refine it based on data.

**RAG (Retrieval-Augmented Generation)**

A technique that combines AI text generation with real-time information retrieval to improve accuracy and relevance.
Instead of guessing, an AI answering a compliance question retrieves the latest regulation from the bank's internal database before generating its response.

**Ring-Fencing**

Separating parts of an organisation to contain risk.
Keeping retail banking isolated from trading desks.
AI undermines this by sharing information instantly across systems.

**Stop-Power**

The authority to slow or halt execution.
Pausing automated withdrawals during a bank run.

**Synchronisation Risk**

Risk that many systems react the same way at the same time.
Multiple banks' AI models sell the same assets simultaneously.

**Tokenised/Programmable Assets**

Assets that carry rules for how they can be used.
Money that can only be spent on rent or food, and expires if unused.

**Trust Layer**

The system that ensures actions are legitimate, authorised, and reversible when needed.
Identity checks, permissions, audit logs, and recourse mechanisms combined.

**Zero Trust**

A security approach that assumes nothing is trusted automatically.
Even employees must constantly re-prove identity and permission before accessing systems.

# Index


**A**

Abdicated Responsibility, 6, 139
Affirm, 89
Afterpay, 89
Agentic AI, 4, 26, 36, 71, 102, 104, 122, 157
AI banking, 40, 45, 101, 146
AI ethics, 136
AI stack, 4, 76–77, 101, 109, 126
Alipay, 71–73
Amazon, 18, 24, 106
AML, 22, 137
Anthropic, 41, 103
Anthropic's Claude Opus 4.6, 41
Apple Pay, 24
Arista, 31
Artificial intelligence. See AI
Asana, 34
Automation Bias, 6, 139, 158

**B**

Basel I, 5, 116
Basel II, 117
Basel III, 5, 116–117, 119–120, 122
Basel V, 5, 118–120, 126
Behavioural loop, 51
Behavioural signals, 80, 83, 98, 105
Blockchain, 27, 58, 163

**C**

Cash management, 54
CeFi, 3, 28, 30
Centralised finance, 29
Chat interfaces, 18, 102
Chat window, 34
Chatbots, 16, 76
Cloud migrations, 145
Collateral, 28–29, 50–52, 81, 97, 105, 131
Collateral shock, 131
Control, 10, 15–16, 22, 24, 27, 30–33, 35, 37–38, 43, 46–47, 50, 54–55, 58, 61–62, 64, 66, 72–80, 82–85, 91, 97, 101, 107, 109–110, 115–116, 119, 128–130, 132, 134, 145, 147, 149–150, 152, 159
Copilots, 18, 32, 75, 102, 148
Core banking replacements, 145
Correlation risk, 56
Credit assessment, 23, 124, 162
Credit decision, 23, 44, 82
Credit engines, 22
CRM rollouts, 145
Cross-border liquidity, 57
Cross-border payments, 60, 63
CrowdStrike, 106
Crypto, 28, 56–58, 108
Cryptoasset, 56

**D**

Data, 4, 15, 22, 24, 27, 31, 33–34, 42–43, 45–46, 54, 69, 73, 76–79, 81–84, 89, 98, 101, 109–110, 120, 124–125, 129, 133, 136–139, 146, 158–159, 161, 163
David Vélez, 22
Decentralisation, 26–27, 66, 110
Decentralised finance, 28

Decision surfaces, 10, 45, 75, 148, 159
DeFi, 3, 27–28, 30, 131
Demis Hassabis, 36, 105
Dependency risk, 130
Deterministic systems, 22
Digital banking, 7, 9, 13–15, 21, 40, 45, 47–48, 79, 87, 99, 101, 145–147
Digital-only bank, 44-45, 146
Drift, 6, 19, 40, 115, 118, 141, 160
Duration mismatch, 49

**E**

e-CNY, 66, 72–73
E-commerce, 23
Encryption, 85
Execution, 3–5, 9, 12, 18, 28–31, 33, 35, 38, 41, 43, 45–46, 48, 53, 55, 57, 60, 62–66, 68, 70–73, 76–77, 79–83, 85, 90–103, 106, 108–111, 116, 118–120, 123–124, 126, 141, 143, 147, 150–155, 157, 160, 162, 164

**F**

Feedback loops, 77, 120
Figma, 34
Fraud systems, 22, 29, 68
Funds Transfer Pricing. See FTP
FX pricing, 91

**G**

GameStop episode, 94
Generation Alpha, 151
Generative AI, 3, 5, 25–26, 35–36, 45, 54, 92, 104, 108, 122, 160
Generative model, 104

**H**

Hedge funds, 94
Herding behaviour, 119
Horizontal tools, 75
Hot money, 51
Human-in-the-loop, 120, 123, 161

**I**

Inference, 33, 57, 76–81, 101, 110, 161
Integration, 9, 43, 79, 92
Internet of Things. See IoT
Internet of Things (IoT), 27, 37
Intraday liquidity loop, 50
IVVI. See identity verification value and information

**J**

Jack Forestell, 69
Joy Buolamwini, 136
JPM Coin, 57
JPMorgan Chase, 49–50, 105, 144

**K**

KakaoBank, 18, 23
Klarna, 89

**L**

Large language models, 36, 78–79, 102, 122
Large-scale cloud, 129
LendingClub, 88
Limit systems, 22
Lineage, 43, 77
Logic-driven agents, 107
Logs, 50, 85, 155, 164

**M**

Machine-readable trust, 85, 162
Market loop, 51
Market-based liquidity, 52
MCP Apps, 24, 34
Michael Miebach, 69
Model Bias, 6, 141
Model Context Protocol, 24, 162
Model Context Protocols. See MCP
Model risk management, 114, 120
Moderna, 18, 33
Money-market funds, 48
MOVEit Transfer, 129
M-Pesa, 4, 10, 74

**N**
Neobanks, 91
Nubank, 10, 17, 22
Nvidia, 31, 33

**O**
Orchestration layer, 25, 34–35, 83, 108, 162–163
Organisational unit, 25, 101, 104

**P**
P2P, 88, 90, 93, 96
PayPal, 4, 70, 107
Peer-to-peer lending platforms, 88
Plumbing, 6, 67, 74, 81, 135, 141–142
Portfolio, 41, 124
Programmable liabilities, 4, 57–58
Project Dunbar, 63
Project Helvetia, 64
Project Icebreaker, 64
Project Jasper–Ubin, 62
Project Jura, 63
Project mBridge, 63

**R**
Recommendation engines, 102
Ring-fencing, 4, 84, 163
Risks marginalisation, 92
Roblox, 106
ROl, 95

**S**
Sam Altman, 36, 75, 105, 127
Separability, 84
Settlement crisis, 131
Silent drift, 141
Silent Value Change, 6, 141
Silicon Valley Bank, 10, 16, 48, 116
Starling Bank, 44
Steve Jobs, 87
Stewardship, 35, 150
Stripe, 4, 70, 105
Supply-chain finance, 37
SWIFT, 66–67
Switching costs, 24

**T**
Tim Berners-Lee, 27
Tokenised deposit, 58
Tokenised treasuries, 48
Trade finance, 57
TradFi, 3, 28, 30
Traditional banks, 19, 24
Traditional finance, 29
Traditional model, 9
Traditional risk frameworks, 115

**U**
Unequal error distribution, 6, 136, 140
Unified Payments Interface. See UPI
Universal Commerce Protocol. See UCP

**V**
Valuation, 56, 91

**W**
WallStreetBets, 94
Web ., 3, 26–27
Web, 3, 26–27
WeBank, 10, 18, 23
WeChat Pay, 71, 73

**Z**
Zero trust, 6, 129–130, 164
Zopa, 88

# References

## Chapter 1

[1] Dimon, Jamie; *Annual Letter to Shareholders*; JPMorgan Chase & Co.; New York; April 2024; *https://www.jpmorganchase.com/ir/annual-report*

[2] Solomon, David; Interview on Artificial Intelligence and Leadership; CNBC; CNBC LLC; Englewood Cliffs; June 2023; *https://www.cnbc.com*

[3] Nu Holdings Ltd.; *Form 20-F Annual Report*; U.S. Securities and Exchange Commission; Washington, D.C.; 2023; *https://ir.nubank.com.br*

[4] Huang, Weizhang; "WeBank's Digital Banking Model"; *Journal of Digital Banking*; Henry Stewart Publications; London; 2021

[5] Lee, Sang-Hun; "KakaoBank's Platform Strategy"; *Korea Economic Daily*; Korea Economic Daily; Seoul; 2022

[6] Moderna, Inc.; "Moderna Launches AI Academy for All Employees," Moderna Media Center, December 9, 2021, *https://www.modernatx.com/media-center/all-media/blogs/moderna-launches-ai-academy-all-employees*

[7] Amazon Web Services; "Moderna: Machine Learning and the mRNA Platform," AWS Case Study, *https://aws.amazon.com/solutions/case-studies/moderna-machine-learning/*

[8] Palantir Technologies; "Gotham Platform Overview," Palantir official website, 2023, *https://www.palantir.com/platforms/gotham/*

[9] Harari, Yuval Noah; *Homo Deus: A Brief History of Tomorrow*; HarperCollins; London; 2016

[10] Vélez, David; "Building Nubank"; *Harvard Business Review*; Harvard Business Publishing; Boston; May–June 2022

[11] WeBank Co. Ltd.; *Annual Report*; WeBank; Shenzhen; 2023; *https://www.webank.com*

[12] KakaoBank Corp.; *Annual Report*; KakaoBank; Seongnam; 2023; *https://www.kakaobank.com*

[13] Daniel, Emmanuel, The Great Transition: The Personalization of Finance is Here, Lafferty Group, Singapore, 2022.

[14] Anthropic; "Introducing the Model Context Protocol"; Anthropic Blog; Anthropic; San Francisco; 2024; *https://www.anthropic.com*

**Chapter 2**

[15] Ullal, Jayshree; Interview; *Bloomberg Technology*; Bloomberg L.P.; New York; 2023

[16] Arista Networks; *Earnings Call Transcript*; Arista Networks Inc.; Santa Clara; 2023

[17] Ullal, Jayshree, "Arista Networks Earnings Call Transcript," Arista Networks Investor Relations, Santa Clara, United States, February 2024, *https://investors.arista.com*

[18] Huang, Jensen; "NVIDIA GTC Keynote"; NVIDIA Corporation; Santa Clara; March 2024; *https://www.nvidia.com/gtc*

[19] OpenAI; "Function Calling and Tool Use in GPT Models"; OpenAI Platform Documentation; OpenAI; San Francisco; 2023; *https://platform.openai.com*

[20] Altman, Sam, "Moore's Law for Everything," Personal Blog, United States, March 2021, *https://moores.samaltman.com*

[21] Hassabis, Demis; "The Path to Artificial General Intelligence"; DeepMind Blog; Google DeepMind; London; 2023; *https://deepmind.com/*

[22] Bengio, Yoshua; "AI and the Risks of Autonomous Systems"; *Frontiers in Artificial Intelligence*; Frontiers Media; Lausanne; 2023

**Chapter 3**

[23] McLuhan, Marshall; *Understanding Media: The Extensions of Man*; McGraw-Hill; New York; 1964

[24] Li, Fei-Fei; Remarks at the World Economic Forum Annual Meeting; World Economic Forum; Geneva; January 2023

[25] Anthropic; "Claude Opus Technical Overview"; Anthropic; San Francisco; 2024; *https://www.anthropic.com*

[26] Boden, Anne; *Banking on It: How I Disrupted an Industry*; Penguin Business; London; 2020

[27] BNY Mellon; "AI for Everyone, Everywhere"; Press Release; BNY Mellon; New York; 2024

[28] Reses, Jackie; Remarks at Money20/20; Money20/20; Amsterdam; October 2023

**Chapter 4**

[29] Huxley, Aldous; *Complete Essays*; Harper & Row; New York; 1958

[30] JPMorgan Chase & Co.; *Investor Day Presentation*; JPMorgan Chase; New York; 2023; *https://www.jpmorganchase.com*

[31] Piepszak, Jennifer; Remarks at Barclays Global Financial Services Conference; Barclays; London; 2023

[32] Bailey, Andrew; "Financial Stability in a Changing World"; Bank of England Speech; Bank of England; London; March 2023; *https://www.bankofengland.co.uk*

[33] Duffie, Darrell; "Intermediation and Liquidity"; *American Economic Review*; American Economic Association; Nashville; May 2012; pp. 49–53

[34] HSBC Holdings plc; "Real-Time Treasury Solutions"; HSBC Corporate Banking Report; HSBC; London; 2023

[35] Citigroup; "Generative AI in Financial Services"; Citi GPS Report; Citigroup; New York; 2024

[36] JPMorgan Chase & Co.; "Onyx and JPM Coin Overview"; JPMorgan Chase; New York; 2023; *https://www.jpmorgan.com*

[37] Standard Chartered Bank, "Tokenised Deposits and Digital Assets Strategy," Press Release, London, United Kingdom, 2023, *https://www.sc.com*

[38] Sidhu, Jay; Interview; *American Banker*; Arizent; New York; 2023

[39] Custodia Bank, "Custodia Bank and Vantage Bank Announce Tokenised Deposit Pilot," Press Release, Cheyenne, United States, 2023, *https://www.custodiabank.com*

**Chapter 5**

[40] Huang, Jensen; Nvidia GTC Keynote; NVIDIA Corporation; San Jose; March 2017

[41] Bank of Canada; "Project Jasper–Ubin: Cross-Border Interbank Payments"; Bank of Canada; Ottawa; 2019

[42] Monetary Authority of Singapore; "Project Ubin Phase 5"; MAS; Singapore; 2019

[43] Banque de France; Swiss National Bank, "Project Jura Final Report," Paris and Zurich, France/Switzerland, December 2021.

[44] Bank for International Settlements; "Project Dunbar"; BIS Innovation Hub; Basel; March 2022

[45] Bank for International Settlements; "Project mBridge"; BIS Innovation Hub; Basel; 2023

[46] Swiss National Bank; "Project Helvetia"; SNB and BIS Report; Zurich; 2020

[47] Bank for International Settlements; "Project Icebreaker"; BIS Innovation Hub; Basel; 2023

[48] SWIFT; "SWIFT Explores Tokenised Assets and Public Blockchain Interoperability"; SWIFT Press Release; Brussels; 2024

[49] Google; "Universal Commerce Protocol Announcement"; Google Developers Blog; Google LLC; Mountain View; 2024

[50] Visa Inc.; Investor Day Transcript; Visa Inc.; Foster City; 2023

[51] Mastercard Inc.; Investor Day Transcript; Mastercard; Purchase; 2023

[52] Chriss, Alex, "PayPal Investor Day Presentation," PayPal Investor Relations, New York, United States, 2024.

[53] Stripe; "Stripe Radar and AI Systems Overview"; Stripe Documentation; Stripe Inc.; San Francisco; 2023; *https://stripe.com*

[54] Reserve Bank of India; *Report on Digital Payments*; RBI; Mumbai; 2023

[55] Reserve Bank of India; *Guidelines on Digital Lending*; RBI; Mumbai; September 2022

[56] People's Bank of China; *Digital Currency Research Progress Report*; PBOC; Beijing; 2023

[57] People's Bank of China; *Progress of Research & Development of e-CNY*; PBOC; Beijing; 2023

[58] Zhu, Feng; Furr, Nathan, The New China Playbook, Harvard Business Review Press, Boston, United States, 2021.

[59] Safaricom PLC; *Annual Report*; Safaricom; Nairobi; 2023

[60] Safaricom PLC, "M-Pesa Super App and AI Integration Strategy," Annual Report, Nairobi, Kenya, 2023, *https://www.safaricom.co.ke*

**Chapter 6**

[61] Altman, Sam; "OpenAI DevDay Keynote"; OpenAI; San Francisco; November 2023; *https://openai.com*

**Chapter 7**

[62] Isaacson, Walter; *Steve Jobs*; Simon & Schuster; New York; 2011

[63] Zopa Bank Ltd., Annual Report, London, United Kingdom, 2023.

[64] LendingClub Corporation, Annual Report (Form 10-K), San Francisco, United States, 2023.

[65] Klarna Bank AB, Annual Report, Stockholm, Sweden, 2023.

[66] Affirm Holdings Inc., Annual Report (Form 10-K), San Francisco, United States, 2023.

[67] Phillips, Matt; "How WallStreetBets Pushed GameStop"; *New York Times*; New York Times Company; New York; January 27, 2021

[68] OpenAI, "Acquisition of ROl Team Announcement," San Francisco, United States, 2024.

[69] OpenAI Blog, "AI for Everyday Life," San Francisco, United States, 2024.

**Chapter 8**

[70] Kander, John; Ebb, Fred, Cabaret, Broadway Musical Script, New York, United States, 1966.

[71] Ng, Andrew; "The Rise of Agentic Workflows"; DeepLearning.AI Newsletter; DeepLearning.AI; Palo Alto; 2024

[72] Anthropic, "Claude 3 and Agent Capabilities Overview," Technical Report, San Francisco, United States, 2024, *https://www.anthropic.com*

[73] Visa Inc., "AI-Powered Risk Management," Annual Report (Form 10-K), Foster City, United States, 2023.

[74] Stripe Inc., "Stripe Radar Machine Learning Overview," Technical Documentation, San Francisco, United States, 2024, *https://stripe.com*

[75] Piepszak, Jennifer, "Liquidity Management in a Real-Time World," JPMorgan Investor Presentation, 2024.

[76] Capital One Financial Corp., Annual Report (Form 10-K), McLean, United States, 2023.

[77] Amazon.com Inc., "AI in Fulfilment Operations," Annual Report, Seattle, United States, 2023.

[78] CrowdStrike Holdings Inc., Annual Report (Form 10-K), Austin, United States, 2023.

[79] Roblox Corporation; "Developer Platform Overview"; Roblox; San Mateo; 2023; *https://developer.roblox.com*

[80] Epic Games, "Unreal Editor for Fortnite (UEFN) Documentation," Cary, United States, 2023, *https://dev.epicgames.com*

**Chapter 9**

[81] Steinbeck, John; *America and Americans*; Viking Press; New York; 1966

[82] Asness, Clifford; "The Siren Song of Factor Timing"; AQR Capital Management; Greenwich; 2017

[83] Basel Committee on Banking Supervision; *Prudential Treatment of Cryptoasset Exposures*; Bank for International Settlements; Basel; December 2022; *https://www.bis.org*

[84] Bank for International Settlements; *Annual Economic Report*; BIS; Basel; June 2023; *https://www.bis.org*

[85] Carstens, Agustín; "Innovation and Financial Stability"; BIS Speech; Bank for International Settlements; Basel; 2023

[86] Financial Stability Board; *Artificial Intelligence and Financial Stability*; FSB; Basel; November 2023; *https://www.fsb.org*

[87] Bank of England; *Machine Learning in UK Financial Services*; Discussion Paper; Bank of England; London; 2022

[88] Cunliffe, Jon, "Financial Stability and the Pace of Change," Bank of England Speech, London, United Kingdom, July 2022.

[89] Bengio, Yoshua, "Managing AI Risks," Nature Machine Intelligence, London, United Kingdom, 2023.

[90] Reserve Bank of India, "Discussion Paper on Digital Lending," Mumbai, India, August 2022.

[91] Central Bank of Kenya, "Digital Credit Market Review," Nairobi, Kenya, 2021.

**Chapter 10**

[92] Sun Tzu; *The Art of War*; Oxford University Press; Oxford; translated by Samuel B. Griffith; 1963

[93] BBC News, "Deepfake Video Scam Costs Firm $25m," London, United Kingdom, February 2024.

[94] Hong Kong Police Force, "Deepfake Fraud Alert," Hong Kong, China, February 2024.

[95] Cybersecurity and Infrastructure Security Agency; "MOVEit Vulnerability Alert"; CISA; Washington, D.C.; June 2023; *https://www.cisa.gov*

[96] Kindervag, John; "Build Security into Your Network's DNA"; Forrester Research; Cambridge; 2010

**Chapter 11**

[97] Berra, Yogi; *The Yogi Book*; Workman Publishing; New York; 1998

[98] Bender, Emily M.; Gebru, Timnit; "On the Dangers of Stochastic Parrots"; *Proceedings of FAccT*; Association for Computing Machinery; New York; March 2021

[99] Buolamwini, Joy; Gebru, Timnit; "Gender Shades"; *Proceedings of Machine Learning Research*; PMLR; 2018

[100] Whittaker, Meredith; "The Steep Cost of Capture"; AI Now Institute Report; New York University; New York; 2018

**Chapter 12**

[101] Broad, William J.; "Richard Garwin Reflects on the Hydrogen Bomb"; *New York Times*; New York Times Company; New York; May 2023

[102] JPMorgan Chase & Co.; "Manuela Veloso Appointed Head of AI Research"; Press Release; JPMorgan Chase; New York; 2022

[103] Heitsenrether, Teresa; Remarks at JPMorgan Investor Day; JPMorgan Chase & Co.; New York; 2023

[104] Goldman Sachs; *2024 Investor Day Transcript*; Goldman Sachs Group Inc.; New York; 2024; *https://www.goldmansachs.com*

[105] Dimon, Jamie; *Annual Letter to Shareholders*; JPMorgan Chase & Co.; New York; April 2023; *https://www.jpmorganchase.com/ir/annual-report*

[106] Fink, Larry; *Annual Letter to Investors*; BlackRock Inc.; New York; March 2023

**Chapter 13**

[107] Eisenhower, Dwight D.; Speech to the National Defense Executive Reserve Conference; Office of the President; Washington, D.C.; November 14, 1957

# Bibliography


Acemoglu, Daron; Restrepo, Pascual; "Automation and New Tasks: How Technology Displaces and Reinstates Labor," *Journal of Economic Perspectives*, Vol. 33, No. 2, 2019.

Adrian, Tobias; Shin, Hyun Song; "Liquidity and Leverage," *Journal of Financial Intermediation*, Vol. 19, No. 3, 2010.

Affirm Holdings Inc.; *Annual Report (Form 10-K)*; San Francisco, United States; 2023.

Altman, Sam; "Moore's Law for Everything"; Personal Blog; (place not stated); March 2021; *https://moores.samaltman.com/*

Altman, Sam; "OpenAI DevDay Keynote"; OpenAI; San Francisco, United States; November 2023; *https://openai.com.*

Amazon.com Inc.; "AI in Fulfilment Operations"; *Annual Report*; Seattle, United States; 2023.

Anthropic; "Claude 3 and Agent Capabilities Overview"; Technical Report; San Francisco, United States; 2024.

Anthropic; "Claude Opus Technical Overview"; Technical Report; San Francisco, United States; 2024.

Anthropic; "Introducing the Model Context Protocol"; Anthropic Blog; San Francisco, United States; 2024.

Arista Networks Inc.; *Earnings Call Transcript*; Santa Clara, United States; 2023.

Asness, Clifford; "The Siren Song of Factor Timing"; AQR Capital Management; Greenwich, United States; 2017.

Bailey, Andrew; "Financial Stability in a Changing World"; Speech; Bank of England; London, United Kingdom; March 2023; *https://www.bankofengland.co.uk*

Bank for International Settlements; *Annual Economic Report*; Basel, Switzerland; 2022–2024.

Bank for International Settlements; *Project Dunbar*; BIS Innovation Hub; Basel, Switzerland; 2022.

Bank for International Settlements; *Project Helvetia*; BIS Innovation Hub; Basel, Switzerland; 2020.

Bank for International Settlements; *Project Icebreaker*; BIS Innovation Hub; Basel, Switzerland; 2023.

Bank for International Settlements; *Project Jura*; BIS Innovation Hub; Basel, Switzerland; 2021.

Bank for International Settlements; *Project mBridge*; BIS Innovation Hub; Basel, Switzerland; 2022–2024.

Bank of Canada; "Project Jasper–Ubin: Cross-Border Interbank Payments"; Ottawa, Canada; 2019

Bank of England; *Machine Learning in UK Financial Services*; Discussion Paper; London, United Kingdom; 2022.

Banque de France; Swiss National Bank; *Project Jura Final Report*; Paris, France and Zurich, Switzerland; December 2021.

Barabási, Albert-László; *Linked: How Everything Is Connected to Everything Else and What It Means*; Cambridge, MA: Perseus Publishing; 2002.

Basel Committee on Banking Supervision; *Prudential Treatment of Cryptoasset Exposures*; Basel, Switzerland: Bank for International Settlements; 2022.

BBC News; "Deepfake Video Scam Costs Firm $25m"; London, United Kingdom; February 2024.

Bender, Emily M.; Gebru, Timnit; McMillan-Major, Angelina; Shmitchell, Shmargaret; "On the Dangers of Stochastic Parrots: Can Language Models Be Too Big?" *Proceedings of the ACM Conference on Fairness, Accountability, and Transparency (FAccT)*; New York, United States: Association for Computing Machinery; 2021.

Beniger, James R.; *The Control Revolution: Technological and Economic Origins of the Information Society*; Cambridge, MA: Harvard University Press; 1986.

Bengio, Yoshua; "Managing AI Risks"; *Nature Machine Intelligence*; London, United Kingdom; 2023.

Bengio, Yoshua; "AI and the Risks of Autonomous Systems"; *Frontiers in Artificial Intelligence*; Lausanne, Switzerland: Frontiers Media; 2023.

Berra, Yogi; *The Yogi Book*; New York, United States: Workman Publishing; 1998.

BNY Mellon; "AI for Everyone, Everywhere"; Press Release; New York, United States; 2024.

Boden, Anne; *Banking on It: How I Disrupted an Industry*; London, United Kingdom: Penguin Business; 2020.

Broad, William J.; "Richard Garwin Reflects on the Hydrogen Bomb"; *The New York Times*; New York, United States; May 2023.

Brunnermeier, Markus K.; Oehmke, Martin; "The Maturity Rat Race"; *Journal of Finance*; 2013.

Brynjolfsson, Erik; McAfee, Andrew; *The Second Machine Age*; New York, United States: W. W. Norton; 2014.

Buolamwini, Joy; *Unmasking AI: My Mission to Protect What Is Human in a World of Machines*; New York, United States: Random House; 2023.

Buolamwini, Joy; Gebru, Timnit; "Gender Shades"; *Proceedings of Machine Learning Research*; 2018.

Capital One Financial Corp.; *Annual Report (Form 10-K)*; McLean, United States; 2023.

Carstens, Agustín; "Innovation and Financial Stability"; Speech; Bank for International Settlements; Basel, Switzerland; 2023.

Central Bank of Kenya; *Digital Credit Market Review*; Nairobi, Kenya; 2021.

Chriss, Alex; "PayPal Investor Day Presentation"; PayPal Investor Relations; United States; 2024.

Citigroup; "Generative AI in Financial Services"; Citi GPS Report; New York, United States; 2024.

Consumer Financial Protection Bureau; guidance on adverse action and explainability under automated decision systems; Washington, D.C., United States; various releases.

CrowdStrike Holdings Inc.; *Annual Report (Form 10-K)*; Austin, United States; 2023.

Cunliffe, Jon; "Financial Stability and the Pace of Change"; Speech; Bank of England; London, United Kingdom; July 2022.

Custodia Bank; "Custodia Bank and Vantage Bank Announce Tokenised Deposit Pilot"; Press Release; Cheyenne, United States; 2023; *https://www.custodiabank.com*

Cybersecurity and Infrastructure Security Agency; "MOVEit Vulnerability Alert"; Washington, D.C., United States; June 2023; *https://www.cisa.gov*

Cyert, Richard M.; March, James G.; *A Behavioral Theory of the Firm*; Englewood Cliffs, United States: Prentice Hall; 1963.

Daniel, Emmanuel; *The Great Transition: The Personalization of Finance is Here*; Singapore: World Scientific Publishing Co. Pte. Ltd.; 2022.

Danielsson, Jon; *The Illusion of Control: Why Financial Crises Happen and What We Can (and Can't) Do About It*; New Haven, United States: Yale University Press; 2022.

Dimon, Jamie; *Annual Letter to Shareholders*; JPMorgan Chase & Co.; New York, United States; 2023; 2024.

Duffie, Darrell; *Dark Markets: Asset Pricing and Information Transmission in Over-the-Counter Markets*; Princeton, United States: Princeton University Press; 2011.

Duffie, Darrell; "Intermediation and Liquidity"; *American Economic Review*; Nashville, United States; May 2012; pp. 49–53.

Eisenhower, Dwight D.; Speech to the National Defense Executive Reserve Conference; Washington, D.C., United States; November 14, 1957.

Epic Games; "Unreal Editor for Fortnite (UEFN) Documentation"; Cary, United States; 2023; *https://dev.epicgames.com*

Farboodi, Maryam; Veldkamp, Laura; "A Model of the Data Economy"; NBER Working Paper; Cambridge, United States; 2020.

Financial Stability Board; *Artificial Intelligence and Financial Stability*; Basel, Switzerland; November 2023; *https://www.fsb.org*

Fink, Larry; *Annual Letter to Investors*; BlackRock Inc.; New York, United States; March 2023.

Floridi, Luciano; *The Ethics of Information*; Oxford, United Kingdom: Oxford University Press; 2013.

Goldman Sachs Group Inc.; *2024 Investor Day Transcript*; New York, United States; 2024.

Google LLC; "Universal Commerce Protocol Announcement"; Google Developers Blog; Mountain View, United States; 2024.

Granovetter, Mark; "Threshold Models of Collective Behavior"; *American Journal of Sociology*, Vol. 83, No. 6; Chicago, United States; 1978.

Harari, Yuval Noah; *Homo Deus: A Brief History of Tomorrow*; London, United Kingdom: Harvill Secker; 2015.

Hassabis, Demis; "The Path to Artificial General Intelligence"; DeepMind Blog; London, United Kingdom; 2023; *https://deepmind.com*

Heitsenrether, Teresa; Remarks at JPMorgan Investor Day; New York, United States; 2023.

Hong Kong Police Force; "Deepfake Fraud Alert"; Hong Kong, China; February 2024.

HSBC Holdings plc; "Real-Time Treasury Solutions"; HSBC Corporate Banking Report; London, United Kingdom; 2023.

Huang, Jensen; "NVIDIA GTC Keynote"; NVIDIA Corporation; Santa Clara, United States; March 2017; March 2024; *https://www.nvidia.com/gtc*

Huang, Weizhang; "WeBank's Digital Banking Model"; *Journal of Digital Banking*; London, United Kingdom: Henry Stewart Publications; 2021.

Huxley, Aldous; *Complete Essays*; New York, United States: Harper & Row; 1958.

Isaacson, Walter; *Steve Jobs*; New York, United States: Simon & Schuster; 2011.

JPMorgan Chase & Co.; "Manuela Veloso Appointed Head of AI Research"; Press Release; New York, United States; 2022.

JPMorgan Chase & Co.; "Onyx and JPM Coin Overview"; New York, United States; 2023; *https://www.jpmorgan.com*

JPMorgan Chase & Co.; Investor Day Presentation; New York, United States; 2023.

KakaoBank Corp.; *Annual Report*; Seongnam, South Korea; 2023.

Kander, John; Ebb, Fred; *Cabaret*; New York, United States; 1966.

Kindervag, John; "Build Security into Your Network's DNA"; Forrester Research; Cambridge, United States; 2010.

Kindleberger, Charles P.; Aliber, Robert Z.; *Manias, Panics, and Crashes: A History of Financial Crises*; 6th ed.; Basingstoke, United Kingdom: Palgrave Macmillan; 2011.

Klarna Bank AB; *Annual Report*; Stockholm, Sweden; 2023.

Lee, Sang-Hun; "KakaoBank's Platform Strategy"; *Korea Economic Daily*; Seoul, South Korea; 2022.

LendingClub Corporation; *Annual Report (Form 10-K)*; San Francisco, United States; 2023.

Lessig, Lawrence; *Code and Other Laws of Cyberspace*; New York, United States: Basic Books; 1999.

Li, Fei-Fei; Remarks at the World Economic Forum Annual Meeting; Geneva, Switzerland; January 2023.

Maersk; "AI and Advanced Analytics in Logistics"; A.P. Møller–Maersk; Copenhagen, Denmark (corporate HQ); 2022; *https://www.maersk.com*

March, James G.; Simon, Herbert A.; *Organizations*; New York, United States: Wiley; 1958.

Mastercard Inc.; Investor Day Transcript; Purchase, United States; 2023.

McLuhan, Marshall; *Understanding Media: The Extensions of Man*; New York, United States: McGraw-Hill; 1964.

Mims, Christopher; "Amazon's AI-Powered Logistics Machine"; *The Wall Street Journal*; New York, United States; 2021.

Monetary Authority of Singapore; "Project Ubin Phase 5"; Singapore; 2019.

Ng, Andrew; "The Rise of Agentic Workflows"; DeepLearning.AI Newsletter; Palo Alto, United States; 2024.

Nu Holdings Ltd.; *Form 20-F Annual Report*; Washington, D.C., United States: U.S. Securities and Exchange Commission; 2023; *https://ir.nubank.com.br*

O'Neil, Cathy; *Weapons of Math Destruction*; New York, United States: Crown; 2016.

OpenAI; "Function Calling and Tool Use in GPT Models"; OpenAI Platform Documentation; San Francisco, United States; 2023; *https://platform.openai.com*

OpenAI; "Acquisition of ROl Team Announcement"; San Francisco, United States; 2024.

OpenAI Blog; "AI for Everyday Life"; San Francisco, United States; 2024.

Palantir Technologies; "Gotham Platform Overview"; Denver, United States (corporate base); 2023; *https://www.palantir.com/platforms/gotham/*

Park, Andrea; "Moderna's AI Strategy Helped It Develop Its Covid-19 Vaccine in Record Time"; *Fierce Pharma*; Washington, D.C., United States; 2021.

People's Bank of China; *Digital Currency Research Progress Report*; Beijing, China; 2023.

People's Bank of China; *Progress of Research & Development of e-CNY*; Beijing, China; 2023.

Phillips, Matt; "How WallStreetBets Pushed GameStop"; *The New York Times*; New York, United States; January 27, 2021.

Piepszak, Jennifer; "Liquidity Management in a Real-Time World"; JPMorgan Investor Presentation; New York, United States; 2024.

Piepszak, Jennifer; Remarks at Barclays Global Financial Services Conference; London, United Kingdom; 2023.

Reserve Bank of India; "Discussion Paper on Digital Lending"; Mumbai, India; August 2022.

Reserve Bank of India; "Guidelines on Digital Lending"; Mumbai, India; September 2022.

Reserve Bank of India; "Report on Digital Payments"; Mumbai, India; 2023.

Reses, Jackie; Remarks at Money20/20; Amsterdam, Netherlands; October 2023.

Roblox Corporation; "Developer Platform Overview"; San Mateo, United States; 2023; *https://developer.roblox.com*

Russell, Stuart; *Human Compatible: Artificial Intelligence and the Problem of Control*; New York, United States: Viking; 2019.

Safaricom PLC; *Annual Report*; Nairobi, Kenya; 2023.

Schneier, Bruce; *Click Here to Kill Everybody: Security and Survival in a Hyper-Connected World*; New York, United States: W. W. Norton; 2018.

Shin, Hyun Song; *Risk and Liquidity*; Oxford, United Kingdom: Oxford University Press; 2010.

Sidhu, Jay; Interview; *American Banker*; New York, United States; 2023.

Solomon, David; Interview on Artificial Intelligence and Leadership; CNBC; Englewood Cliffs, United States; June 2023.

Standard Chartered Bank; "Tokenised Deposits and Digital Assets Strategy"; Press Release; London, United Kingdom; 2023; *https://www.sc.com*

Steinbeck, John; *America and Americans*; New York, United States: Viking Press; 1966.

Stripe Inc.; "Stripe Radar and AI Systems Overview / Machine Learning Overview"; Stripe Documentation; San Francisco, United States; 2023–2024.

Sun Tzu; *The Art of War*; Oxford, United Kingdom: Oxford University Press; translated by Samuel B. Griffith; 1963.

SWIFT; "SWIFT Explores Tokenised Assets and Public Blockchain Interoperability"; Press Release; Brussels, Belgium; 2024.

Taleb, Nassim Nicholas; *Antifragile: Things That Gain from Disorder*; New York, United States: Random House; 2012.

Thompson, James D.; *Organizations in Action*; New York, United States: McGraw-Hill; 1967.

Ullal, Jayshree; "Arista Networks Earnings Call Transcript"; Arista Networks Investor Relations; Santa Clara, United States; February 2024; *https://investors.arista.com*

Ullal, Jayshree; Interview; Bloomberg Technology; New York, United States; 2023.

Vélez, David; "Building Nubank"; *Harvard Business Review*; Boston, United States; May–June 2022.

Visa Inc.; "AI-Powered Risk Management"; *Annual Report (Form 10-K)*; Foster City, United States; 2023.

Visa Inc.; Investor Day Transcript; Foster City, United States; 2023.

Watts, Duncan J.; *Six Degrees: The Science of a Connected Age*; New York, United States: W. W. Norton; 2003.

WeBank Co. Ltd.; *Annual Report*; Shenzhen, China; 2023; *https://www.webank.com*

Weick, Karl E.; *Sensemaking in Organizations*; Thousand Oaks, United States: Sage Publications; 1995.

Weick, Karl E.; Sutcliffe, Kathleen M.; *Managing the Unexpected: Sustained Performance in a Complex World*; 2nd ed.; Hoboken, United States: Wiley; 2007.

Whittaker, Meredith; "The Steep Cost of Capture"; AI Now Institute Report; New York, United States: New York University; 2018.

Winner, Langdon; "Do Artifacts Have Politics?" *Daedalus*, Vol. 109, No. 1; Cambridge, United States: MIT Press (journal publisher); 1980.

Zhu, Feng; Furr, Nathan; *The New China Playbook*; Boston, United States: Harvard Business Review Press; 2021.

Zopa Bank Ltd.; *Annual Report*; London, United Kingdom; 2023.

Zuboff, Shoshana; *The Age of Surveillance Capitalism*; New York, United States: PublicAffairs; 2019.

www.ingramcontent.com/pod-product-compliance
Lightning Source LLC
LaVergne TN
LVHW050934210926
848482LV00013B/606
* 9 7 9 8 9 0 3 4 2 3 1 6 3 *